HOW RUSSIA
GOT THAT WAY

© 2025, Griffiin Edwards

Cover illustration integrates original royalty-free illustrations by Evgeny Turaev (bear) and Indos82 (double-headed eagle), both sourced on Dreamstime.com.

All rights reserved. Work may not be reproduced in any manner without the expressed, written permission of the copyright holder. For permission to reproduce selections from this book, contact the publisher at the address below.

ISBN 978-1-880100-59-2

Russian Life Books
73 Main Street, Suite 402
Montpelier, VT 05601-0567
russianlife.com
orders@russianlife.com
phone 802-223-4955

HOW RUSSIA GOT THAT WAY

Russian History and Why It Matters

By Griffin Edwards

russian life
BOOKS

For Eliza and Gideon.

Tolle legge.

CONTENTS

INTRODUCTION 7
ORIGINATION: THE MYSTERIOUS BEGINNINGS OF A MYSTERIOUS LAND 12
FOUNDATION: KIEVAN' RUS 22
SUBJUGATION: RUS' AND TATAR TRIBUTE 35
SANCTIFICATION AND CENTRALIZATION:
MUSCOVITE SUPREMACY AND THE TIME OF TROUBLES 45
MODERNIZATION: RUSSIA IN THE IMAGE OF PETER AND CATHERINE 60
INTROSPECTION: IMPERIAL IDENTITY 74
ADAPTATION: REFORMS AND COUNTER-REFORMS 89
DISSOLUTION, CONFUSION, AND REVOLUTION: THE END OF THE ROMANOVS 99
CREATION: THE COMMUNIST EXPERIMENT 108
STAGNATION: THE COLD WAR AND THE END OF THE COMMUNIST DREAM 125
RE-LEGITIMIZATION: AFTER THE END OF HISTORY 135
INTERPRETATION: TODAY'S RUSSIAN PAST 143
APPLICATION: UKRAINE 150
EPILOGUE 158

ACKNOWLEDGMENTS 163
BIBLIOGRAPHY 164
ABOUT THE AUTHOR 173

MAPS

THE RUSSIAN FEDERATION 10
HOW RUSSIA GREW 58

INTRODUCTION

When I was a teenager, my high school had a sister institution in St. Petersburg, Russia. Each year, our school sent a contingent of students to meet with our Russian counterparts, visit their homes, and get a dose of international cultural experience. To a 16-year-old Southern California kid, Russia seemed like the opposite of everything I knew. I applied to join the trip and was thrilled when I was accepted.

A schoolmate and I were tasked with concocting a history lesson for the Russian teens we would meet. We had an idea: Rather than present tidbits from American history, why not open up the floor to discussion and see what happened? We wanted less lecture and more dialogue, so we centered our talk on a common touchstone, the Second World War. We figured this would be something the Russian students had grown up hearing about probably as much as we Americans had. Surely we would hear a parallel rehash of the story we already knew. After all, America and Russia had been allies, so we could draw on that historic friendship to compare notes.

We had wildly underestimated the richness of the conversation we were opening up. The Russian students had grown up inundated with World War II, and their perspective was completely different from ours. It was an almost unrecognizable tale. Rather than a narrative of heroic effort, logistical planning, and America rescuing a helpless, war-torn Europe, their story was one of gritty survival, bloody sacrifice, and heroic loss. They'd never heard of D-Day. We'd never heard of the Battle of Kursk.

As the years went by, the exchange stuck with me. Through college and graduate school, where I dove deeper into the study of Russia, its history, and its language, I kept returning to this conversation, this paradox of a single event retold in wildly different ways.

Unsurprisingly, my experience was not something new. For centuries, scholars have been discussing how history works and what it does. History, we know, is the glue that binds a nation together. The tales societies tell about themselves reveal their values, goals, and culture. Stories, symbols, and collective memories are unifying things, and those who can control how the past is presented can wield immense power. History is dynamic, and the retellings, errors, forgettings, and revisions are just as important as the actual facts, if not more so. The creation of a robust historical memory is critical for a functioning state.[1]

With this in mind, the retelling of history is the best way to understand Russia today.

We in the West are often confused by Russia, our vision clouded by stereotypes and cliches: bears, vodka, tracksuits, buxom blonde spies, nesting dolls. Somewhere at its center is an ex-KGB officer whose opponents keep dying under mysterious circumstances. Russia fascinates and amazes. It is almost more of a living meme, an ethereal parody-land, than it is a real place with real people living real lives. We are most intimately acquainted with it through James Bond, *Call of Duty*, and dashcam videos. It is equal parts mirage, fantasy, and archetype.

So the best way to cut through this haze of stereotypes and preconceptions is to view Russia in the context of its history. Yet not just history as fact, but also, and more importantly, history as myth. By looking at how Russia has sought to reshape its past, we gain a much deeper understanding of why Russia is just so... different.

A Few Notes

This work follows a roughly chronological course. I begin with Russian prehistory and end in the present. This provides threads to follow and themes to hold on to, making it easier to see the full picture. At times I stop to discuss the historical memory of certain subjects. Each chapter is roughly centered on a single touchstone theme for that period.

I conclude with a chapter discussing the ideology of the modern Russian state ("Putinism") and its connection with this history, looking especially at how history informs the Kremlin's actions. I then use the ongoing conflict between Ukraine and Russia as a case study of the ways today's Russia continues to leverage history.

No book on Russia is complete without an obligatory comment on how the author transliterates the Russian language; after all, Russian uses its own alphabet for a set of sounds not easily shoehorned into Latin letters. For this I opted for simplicity: no awkward double letters and deference to common spelling that still reflects Russian phonetics. Thus, "Dostoevsky" not "Dostoyevskiy" and "Romanov" not "Romanoff." Conveniently, this means that Russian words are pronounced as they are written, so even without any Russian-language knowledge, if sounded out, approximate pronunciation is achievable.

Lastly, a note on notes; that is, footnotes. I have tried to minimize their use throughout. Often, I use them for parenthetical information that does not fit neatly into the text but is an interesting aside. When simply giving background information or building the narrative, I have left out footnotes, as this information can be found in multiple places and is fairly widely known, and I merely present it here in a new context and build with it towards new

---

1. See, for instance: Renan, "What is a Nation?"; Durkheim, "From *The Elementary Forms of Religious Life*"; Halbwachs, *On Collective Memory*; and Assmann and Czaplicka, "Collective Memory and Cultural Identity."

meaning. My main sources for this kind of information include *Freeze, Russia: A History*, *The Cambridge History of Russia*, and Billington, *The Icon and the Axe*. but almost any book on Russian history will contain the general outline and established facts relayed here. Notes in the final few chapters, which discuss political arguments and specific news items, are more common than elsewhere. A comprehensive list of sources can be found in the bibliography, listing all the articles, links, and books that have influenced this work. This includes those cited and also many more. My hope is that this approach makes for clearer and easier reading undistracted by superscript numbers.

1

ORIGINATION: THE MYSTERIOUS BEGINNINGS OF A MYSTERIOUS LAND

A traveler | Russian geography | The first peoples of Russia | A collision with Constantinople | The formation of Rus'

The year is AD 921.

A figure sits, hunched and swaying, on the back of a two-humped camel. He can hardly see, let alone speak or move, wrapped as he is in layers of furs and blankets to keep out the cold. Still, the frigid winter wind blows off the Volga steppe and straight to his core. He is miserable, more used to having the blistering Mesopotamian sun on his face than stinging snow in his eyes. But he and his caravan continue on, the only sound the whistling wind and the crunch of camels' feet in dry snow and dead grass.

This is Ahmad ibn Fadlan, a royal diplomat from Baghdad, the glittering capital of the Abbasid Caliphate, which is enjoying a golden age of science, art, medicine, and architecture. He has been sent on a religious mission to the Volga Bulgars, a newly converted tribe on the far reaches of the known world. The Caliph in Baghdad has sent ibn Fadlan to instruct the Bulgars on Muslim devotion. He has already traveled arduously for months through deserts, over mountains, and up rivers, navigating uncharted wilds at the edge of the known world.

When ibn Fadlan arrives among the Bulgars, he is disgusted. The town is ramshackle and filthy, its people barbaric, the weather inhospitable. Still, he sticks to his mission, patiently guiding his eager pupils on how to properly bathe, pray, and act as Muslims. He dines with the Bulgar king with all the decorum and restraint of a practiced envoy. All the while, he makes careful notes on the people and their culture to relay back to the Caliph.[2]

Late one winter night, lingering around a fire in a Bulgar palace, he hears tales about another people far to the northwest, a trading society the Bulgars view with wariness. Rumors say they are huge, fearsome, warlike men, covered in strange tattoos. They hold public orgies in the streets. Their savage warriors thirst for blood. When their chiefs die, they burn them on their riverboats, surrounded by their possessions and accompanied by a slave girl for the

---

2. Ibn Fadlan, *Ibn Fadlan and the Land of Darkness*.

afterlife. Their greatest city lies on a lake island that takes three days to traverse on foot. Woe to the traveler that should encounter them.

This rumored people is called the *Rusiyyah*.

WHEN AHMAD IBN Fadlan encountered the Bulgars[3] and their towns, when he heard these rumors and breathlessly took them back to Baghdad with him, Russia as a state did not exist. But its people had begun to coalesce along the slow-moving rivers criss-crossing the plains, forests, and steppes west of the Ural Mountains.

Russia is large. It is divided into two unequal parts by the Urals, which run north-south. Anything east of this line is considered Asia; anything west, Europe. Even the approximately one-sixth of Russia's land west of these mountains would make it the largest country in Europe. This western realm is the real "homeland" of the Russians, where most of the action happens for much of Russian history.

Naturally, European Russia itself varies in geography. In the far north, near the cities of Murmansk and Arkhangelsk, the climate is near-Arctic, with tall pine forests, boggy terrain, and long winters. In fact, much of the ground of northern Russia is "permafrost": it stays hard and frozen year-round. Even St. Petersburg, sprawling along the marshy Baltic Sea shore, is so close to the pole that there is a stretch of time in winter when the sun never truly rises, and a week in the summer is celebrated as "White Nights": a 24-hour sunlit dream where the concept of time fades away into a surreal, interminable limbo.

The land around St. Petersburg is low-lying, wet, and swampy, with few hills. It was scraped flat by the last Ice Age, leaving behind fertile soil. Just east of the city is Lake Ladoga, the largest freshwater lake in Europe. Several rivers, like the Neva and Volkhov, flow northwest into the White and Baltic Seas. These are slow and deep, ideal for navigation and transportation. Much of the land is covered in forests of birch, larch, and fir.

Five hundred miles south, past Moscow, trees thin out to form more of a plain, connecting this part of Russia with a belt of steppe that stretches from Hungary to China. This land is perfect for agriculture and has for centuries produced abundant crops, most notably wheat. The Volga and Don, also large rivers ideal for navigation, enter the Caspian and Black Seas, flowing south. Weather here can fluctuate from hot, dry summers to frigid winters, with little protection on the sweeping grasslands.

To the west, European Russia borders Ukraine and Belarus. To the south, the forbidding Caucasus[4] Mountains form a natural barrier with Azerbaijan and Georgia. Southwest is the Black Sea; in the North is the Arctic Ocean; and, to the east, of course, are the Ural Mountains.

---

3. It is believed that today's Bulgars are descended from the Volga Bulgars who emigrated into the Balkan region in the later medieval period, founding the nation of Bulgaria.

4. To this day, White people are called "Caucasian" after the inhabitants of this mountain range. In 1795, German anthropologist Johann Friedrich Blumenbach visited the area and, after being impressed by the strength, beauty, and passion of the inhabitants (communities of mountain shepherds), decided to flatter himself and all the people of his home continent by arguing that these were their remaining ancestors. This, of course, is bunk.

Beyond the Urals is the vast land known as Siberia. The very name evokes desolation and exile; Siberia is infamous for gulag prison camps, hermits, and bears, thereby making it, in the public imagination, the most Russian part of Russia. The region – especially its northern reaches – is sparsely populated. But it contains abundant natural resources, such as gold, precious minerals, timber, coal, and oil.[5] In the northern reaches of Siberia, there is even a surprisingly thriving mammoth ivory industry, harvested from giant Ice Age creatures today found mummified in permafrost. Cities and towns dot the map, but with nothing of the density of those encountered west of the Urals.

In sum: Russia is huge. It stretches across 11 time zones, crosses two continents, is lapped by three oceans, and borders nations as diverse as Azerbaijan, Poland, Mongolia, Finland, and Kazakhstan. It has a varied landscape, ranging from arid deserts to high mountains to frozen tundra.

Based on size alone, some might consider Russia a great and formidable power. But the world's largest country started from rather humble beginnings.

ANCIENT MYTH HAS it that, in those murky days before time, three brothers named Lech, Czech, and Rus' were out hunting in the great forests of Eastern Europe. Each saw different prey and fired their arrows at them, leading each hunter in a different direction. Lech went north, Czech south, and Rus' east. Each soon found a promising spot to settle down with their families and herds. Lech founded the Polish nation, Czech the Czech, and Rus' the Russian. Thus did the three peoples of the ethnic group known as the Slavs go forth, become fruitful, and multiply. Eventually, the Slavs populated much of Eastern Europe, including not just Poland, Russia, and the Czech Republic, but also Serbia, Ukraine, Slovakia, Slovenia, and Croatia, sharing many linguistic and cultural similarities.

In reality, though, Russia rose slowly and organically, over centuries, at a veritable crossroads of humanity, with Central Asia and the Fertile Crescent to the south, China to the east, Scandinavia to the north, and Europe to the west. Due to this central location, in prehistory, the lands that are now Russia saw a good deal of human traffic as groups passed through its flatlands. A few even stayed. From its beginning, Russia was not occupied by a single homogenous tribe of people. Rather, several different groups made their way through and built their homes on the lands we today define as Russia.

Limited archaeological evidence points to small tribes settling northern European Russia long before ibn Fadlan's journey. What evidence we have shows that the tribes came mainly from the regions around the Baltic Sea, the Urals, and Central Europe, forming settlements to farm, fish, and raise cattle. Rivers were key sites for migration and human activity. They not only provided water for cooking and fish for food, but also functioned as a major means of transportation for goods and people between the ocean and interior. Family units in villages

---

5. While in English, we usually refer to the entirety of Asian Russia from the Urals to the Pacific Ocean as "Siberia," for Russians, there is one more geographic region at play. The sparse and small settlements along the Pacific coast, near China and Japan, are considered part of the "Russian Far East."

likely lived in large buildings that combined the uses of barns and homes, housing multiple generations and livestock under one roof. These homes were a defense against a winter that might otherwise kill a family's animals, but also a custom that made good hygiene a challenge.

Because these early people did not use writing, lived in small settlements, and much of their tools and other belongings were made of wood that decayed easily, we know very little about what their life was like. We do know that, at times, settlements arose that incorporated multiple groups in distinct quarters, and sometimes nomadic tribes settled for a period to trade with passing interlopers. All we can say for certain is that the evidence suggests that European Russia was sparsely populated with no central authority but criss-crossed by trails used by nomads and traders.

Through ancient times, while Egypt, Greece, and Rome rose and fell, the heartland of Russia remained largely desolate and uncivilized, simply off the map. For the Mediterranean peoples, the interior was terra incognita, land untravelled, home to monsters. But more southerly parts of Russia saw greater activity. Nomadic, pastoral horse-riding groups from Turkish and Eurasian regions, far to the east, were present in what is now southern Russia

A chariot found in a burial site attributed to the Pazyryks, one of the many nomadic societies that occupied Russian lands deep in its past. A photograph by the State Hermitage Museum.

and Ukraine. These groups used the wide steppe as a means to travel across Eurasia in search of pasture and trade.

Indeed, the Black Sea, in what is now Russia's far south, came into heavy contact with Mediterranean cultures, albeit still as a periphery. Greek-style anchors dating back to as early as the Bronze Age (3300 to 1200 BC) have been found on the Black Sea floor, indicating that these waters were by then well-traveled by ancient mariners. Hellenic trading outposts and colonies established by large Greek city-states dotted the Crimean Peninsula and Russia's Black Sea coast. These settlements were specifically designed to ship luxury goods and bountiful commodities back to the mother cities, but often the colonies were so remote as to be autonomous kingdoms in their own right. Power struggles and trade competition led to both lucrative commerce and bloody clashes with native groups. These towns were beacons of high Greek culture in barbarian lands, complete with all the amenities of the Aegean, but far removed from the Peloponnesian homeland.[6]

Before long, these lands became permanently attached to the Greek imagination. The eastern coast of the Black Sea, a vacation destination in today's Russia, is the land where the mythical Jason found the Golden Fleece. Further, the native Scythians' fierce, mounted warrior society likely gave rise to stories of athletic female Amazons. There is indeed evidence that tribes in this region fielded a remarkably high proportion of female fighters.

The Black Sea colonies, originally founded by the Greeks, later passed to the Roman and, from there, Byzantine Empire. Eventually, they comprised the trade routes that were early Russia's main conduit to the wider Mediterranean, Middle Eastern, and European world. Generally speaking, though, Russia was bypassed by the dynamic days of the great civilizations. And with no existing written records from the area dating from this period, there is uncertainty about the people that constituted the land that makes up Russia today, despite the handful of treasures archaeologists have found.

Regardless, the lands and peoples of early Russia would be heavily influenced not so much by the Greeks and Romans, but rather by their Dark Age descendants: the Byzantines.

Russia's early story is deeply colored by its ties with the Byzantine Empire. At the same time, though, this eastern state is often overshadowed, glossed over, in Western histories. This is perhaps the earliest fundamental divergence between the Russian and Western worldview.

We in the West often conceive of our civilization as coming from the ancient Greeks and Romans. Our cities and architecture emulate theirs, our most popular religions (Catholic Christianity and its offshoot, Protestantism) come from them, and much of our philosophy and ideology comes out of the Renaissance and Enlightenment, which were informed, fundamentally, by ancient Greek and Roman sources rediscovered in the early modern period. In a sense, one can easily draw a direct civilizational line from almost any Western society

---

6. See Ascherson, *Black Sea*.

straight back to Athens and Rome. The West's Greco-Roman influences are so ubiquitous that we are often simply unaware of them.

The Byzantine Empire breaks this continuity and is therefore not part of the Western arc. Since it has had few influences on our everyday lives, we find it harder to envision it or include it into our perspective of world history. Yet we should think of Russia as a product of Byzantine civilization, in a manner similar to how we think of the West as descending from Greek and Roman tradition.

Some historical background is necessary.

In the fourth century AD, the massive Roman Empire, groaning under internal and external pressures, was split in two to better administrate and defend it. This created the Western Roman Empire, centered in Rome, and the Eastern Roman Empire, centered on Constantinople, formerly Byzantium and today known as Istanbul. The Eastern Roman Empire occupied territory in the eastern Mediterranean, Anatolia, and the Balkan Peninsula. While Western Rome famously fell to invaders in AD 476, the Eastern Roman Empire continued to thrive. It lasted almost a millennium longer, until 1453, when Constantinople fell to the Ottoman Turks. The Eastern Roman Empire, which a 16th-century historian termed "Byzantine" (the Byzantines called themselves "Romans" and their empire "New Rome"),[7] has a fascinating history in its own right, replete with colorful characters and enchanting intrigue.[8]

After the fall of Rome, Constantinople became the home of classical learning and a beacon of Christianity in the East. At its peak in the middle of the European "Dark Ages," the Byzantine Empire was one of the largest, wealthiest, and most powerful states on Earth. For centuries, it was the major power in the eastern Mediterranean and Middle East. Constantinople, with its soaring Eastern Orthodox churches and sprawling palaces, was a major trade entrepôt, a true crossroads of East and West, situated between the Mediterranean, mainland Europe, and the Black Sea, Middle East, Africa, and India and China. It was truly the center of the known world, with a busy shipping port and ancient paved Roman roads radiating outward from it. Over its lifetime, the Byzantine Empire developed a distinct artistic, religious, and political culture, one with echoes in modern Russia.

Understanding the Byzantines as having been present at the time of Russia's formation (in the late ninth century), and as a civilization that had close cultural, religious, and political ties to Russia, is critical to understanding the Russian context. Early Russians called Byzantium's capital "Tsargrad" – the city of emperors.

---

7. Of course, Roman heritage is a valuable thing, and Byzantium's claim to Rome did not go uncontested. In AD 800, the Frankish king Charlemagne noticed that the Eastern Roman Empire was ruled by an empress, Irene. This was inconceivable, so Charlemagne worked with the pope to have himself crowned Holy Roman Emperor, controlling much of modern France and Germany. Yet this Roman inheritance was tenuous, snatched up merely to glorify Charlemagne and his lands. Hence French Enlightenment philosopher Voltaire's quip that the Holy Roman Empire was "neither holy, nor Roman, nor an empire."

8. For a fascinating, comprehensive, and thoroughly readable history of Byzantium, see Fidler, *Ghost Empire*.

Russians first enter the written historical record through Byzantine eyes. They appear 100 years before ibn Fadlan's trek, although not by name. A ninth-century saintly tale records a raid from strange, pagan, sailing barbarians from the riverlands north of the Black Sea.[9] These people pulled ashore near Constantinople, raided savagely for a while and besieged the city, then retreated back home suddenly, cutting short their rowdy pillaging. The chronicle attributes this to a divine miracle: the emperor and his army were away on campaign, so the city was the raiders' for the taking. The chronicle writer's tone is breathless, bewildered. Who were these strange folk, and what did they want? Were the attackers Norse raiders, or something else Constantinople had never encountered before? The Byzantines could not have known that, at the same time, far outside their borders, a Russian state was beginning to form.

ANCIENT RUSSIA'S RIVERS did not only attract peaceful nomads looking to put down roots or passing through to somewhere else. There was money to be made on these waterways, resources and riches to be exploited. And so it was outsiders, attracted by wealth, who first founded what would become the Russian state.

Between 800 and 1050, the Scandinavian farmers and fishermen known as the Vikings took to the seas, navigating, trading, and settling in the Mediterranean, British Isles, and even the New World. As they traveled, their longships, perfectly engineered for shore and river operations, picked their way expertly up the Volkhov, Don, and Volga through today's European Russia, searching for new trade opportunities and places to settle. It was on one of these journeys that a Viking warlord named Rurik and his band of adventurers first came across the settlement of Novgorod in AD 862.

The citizens of Novgorod, where the River Volkhov enters Lake Ilmen, had found prosperity from their strategic location on a major riverine trade route. The outpost had become a large trading town, home to a diverse community that drew together Slavic peoples and those of various ethnic groups from around the region. Yet they lacked protection, a perilous position for wealthy merchants. The tribes who lived in this settlement therefore requested that warrior-explorer-trader Rurik and his younger brothers settle down and rule over them in exchange for some of their wealth. Rurik's family agreed to the deal. Rurik took control of Novgorod, and his brothers ruled two nearby towns. A few years later, when the brothers died, Rurik became prince of the whole area, eventually extending his power across the land. And so Rurik established Russia.

This is the popular retelling, enshrouded in myth, and it is also more or less in line with the medieval account of the occurrence. However, historians have in recent years interrogated the narrative in an effort to uncover what really happened. Some argue that Rurik was just one in a line of Viking rulers who happened to be in the area, and that he pushed out competing warlords for his slice of the pie. In this framing, Rurik's deal with the Novgorodians is more of a protection racket meant to ensure that the people of the town would pay tribute to Rurik

---

9. Jenkins et al, *Life of St. George of Amastris*.

and his entourage in exchange for security from themselves and rival warlords. Regardless, the people of Novgorod made a deal with Rurik and his family, allowing the foreign interlopers to rule over them.

And this is significant: the Russians of Novgorod invited someone to rule over them. Here, in the very beginning of the story of Russia, we see a sort of consent of the governed. The Novgorodians choose their ruler, laying out the expectations for Rurik and his line as a quid pro quo that was only valid so long as both sides were upheld. Rurik, in the legend, did not invade or conquer; his people were not occupiers. The fact that Rurik and his

Viktor Vasnetsov's 19th-century depiction of Rurik and his brothers accepting payment from the Novgorodians as thanks for using their battle-axes against their enemies instead of against them.

family were invited and not imposed flies in the face of the usual understanding of Russia as inevitably autocratic. And so, already in Russia's foundational legend, there is a tinge of political implication.

Regardless, Russia now built a ruling class. It was made up of nobles, called "boyars" in the Russian tradition, and a government structure that unified a handful of settlements in northwestern Russia. Nobles and other government officials were likely relatives and Norse countrymen of Rurik, the bands with whom he had encountered Novgorod and the other Russian towns. The larger indigenous populace was probably largely Slavic in ethnicity but with other communities mixed in. Over time, however, intermarriage caused distinctions to melt away into a single language and culture. Persistent Scandinavian influence was evident in the new name for the inhabitants of this land: Rus'.[10] The word is possibly derived from the Old Norse "ruotsi," meaning "men who row," a nod to the prowess with which Vikings and their new subjects navigated their longboats through Russia's languid rivers. It could also betray a link to the Swedish regions of Roslagen or Roden.

Mystery surrounds those early years. Most of what we know about the start of Russian history comes from a set of chronicles written hundreds of years after the fact, so our grasp on the finer points is shaky.[11] It is inevitable that there were simplifications, omissions, and revisions made to tell the story a certain way and emphasize specific points more relevant to the audience the authors were writing for. Scholars today are not even sure who exactly wrote these works, whether they were commissioned by rulers, written by and handed down through monks, or done by an educated noble as a side project. And, once more, archaeology is little help, especially when it comes to more abstract concepts like government structure and cultural beliefs that leave scant physical evidence.

In any event, Rurik's successors, Igor and Oleg, further expanded Rus' territory to the south, capturing the town of Kiev (today the capital of Ukraine)[12] and making it their capital. Kiev, too, sat squarely on a trade route, situated on a promontory overlooking the wide Dnieper and bringing commerce from the Black Sea inland. Novgorod remained the second city of the princedom, and the state was probably solidified by the year 900. While the exact details and methods are lost to time, the family and descendants of Rurik spread their rule throughout the region. Today this state is referred to as Kievan Rus'.

This marks the establishment of Russia's first dynasty: the *Rurikovichi*, or Rurikids, the "Sons of Rurik." Each Rus' settlement with its surrounding farmland and towns was headed by a different family member, a prince. All the princes were nominally subservient to the Grand Prince in Kiev. In practice, though, the individual princes could rule with a wide degree of independence, even as the Grand Prince held the most military power, economic clout, and international prestige. The cities ruled by Rurik's descendants not only made up much of Russia proper; their influence spread into what is now Belarus and Ukraine, and these countries today also claim Rurik as their founding father. After all, it was *Kievan* Rus'.

---

10. The apostrophe here denotes a soft *s*, an unfortunate byproduct of transliteration from Russian spelling which has no equivalent in English. Put simply, the *s* sound here is not a harsh consonant. The pronunciation would be closer to "Rooss" than "Rooz."

11. Interestingly, some of these chronicles record not only Russian history but world history, from the biblical creation of the Earth through the Flood and into the current day. As such, years are counted from the exact day of Creation, placing medieval times squarely in the 6000s.

12. Russians spell and pronounce the city "Kiev" ("Key-yev"), while their Ukrainian counterparts spell it "Kyiv" ("Keev"). Both are correct, since they are being transliterated from different languages and alphabets. The "Kyiv" spelling, however, has become more widespread in the West since the start of Russia's full-scale invasion of Ukraine in February 2022 as a show of solidarity with the Ukrainian people. Still, I opt for "Kiev" to maintain consistency with Russian transliterations here.

In sum, Rurik's Kievan Rus' had unified the land, bringing the trade cities under a single family. In taking control of centers like Novgorod, Kiev, and their environs, a Viking adventurer had established what would one day become the Russia we know.

AS IBN FADLAN turned his camel from the Bulgar village, waving one last time at the children as they scurried back to their parents after yelling goodbye, did he contemplate the Rusiyyah? Perhaps he halted his mount on a low rise and studied the snaking Volga flowing slowly below, letting his eyes drift towards the northwestern horizon, across the undulating steppe. Hundreds of miles away was the mythical island capital, those strange and dangerous people with their animalistic customs, whose river navigation skills were legendary. Perhaps he thought of a return trip, or an extended detour to see them with his own eyes. Maybe his Bulgar expedition had whetted his appetite for travel. Sure, it might be cold, but it would be another land to discover...

It was not to be. Ahmad ibn Fadlan returned home to Baghdad, retracing the tradeways down the Volga, across the mountains, and back to the Caliphate, his civilized homeland. The account of his trip remains one of the earliest written records of the Russian people and a remarkable look at how their neighbors saw ancient Rus'.

2

FOUNDATION: KIEVAN' RUS

Vladimir picks Orthodoxy | Rus' united and divided | Novgorodian "democracy" | An iconic battle

Ahmad ibn Fadlan saw the Rus' as occupying a periphery, out of reach of the known world, obscured through rumors carried over hundreds of miles. From another perspective, though, the Rus' were becoming a center. Now that a central authority had coalesced in the ninth century, they were a meeting point for the major world cultures of their day. It was this collision of disparate peoples that shaped the life of Kievan Rus' from the start, creating something altogether new: the foundations of true Russian nationhood.

To the north and west, Norse Viking influence stretched from the Baltic Sea to Britain to Sicily, with tendrils in America. To the south, the Byzantine Empire covered much of the eastern Mediterranean, and ibn Fadlan's Abbasid Caliphate was at this time a major power in the Middle East. Thus, Rus' found itself sandwiched between several neighbors that were wealthy and powerful. Add to this a land easily traversed by deep and slow rivers, and Rurik's line, once it had established control, attracted great wealth. Anyone taking their wares from the Mediterranean or Middle East to the Baltic could forgo a circuitous ocean passage for an easier inland route.

Archaeological artifacts of the time unearthed in modern Russia paint a picture of a land profoundly more cosmopolitan than we might expect. Finds include Arab coins, Byzantine wine jars, and jewelry from Western Europe. Local goods could add value to this trade, too. In the woods just outside Russian towns were abundant sources of luxurious furs and sweet honey. Salt, farmed from local mineral springs, provided a better preservative for pelts than the oft-used alternative, human urine (for obvious reasons). Tall, blond locals captured in battle made excellent slaves. A typical voyage making the trip from "the Varangians [Vikings] to the Greeks [Byzantines]" passed through the cities of the Rurikids, making stops and trading goods at Novgorod, Kiev, and points in between. Boats carrying international travelers and their wares plying up and down the rivers were a common sight.

As people traveled these routes, so too did their cultures. Among the most major influences, if not the most significant, to result from this exchange was Orthodox Christianity.

Orthodoxy became a defining feature of Russian culture that ties it to Byzantium to this day. But the adoption of Orthodoxy was not inevitable. If anything, it was unlikely.

IN 978, VLADIMIR I was crowned Grand Prince of the Rus'. Ruling from the capital in Kiev, he oversaw all the boyars and the lower Rurikovich prices of the various cities of Rus'.

He did not take the throne lightly. His rise to power had not been straightforward. Following the Norse custom, the eldest son of a ruler might not be the chief inheritor of a dead ruler's realm. Instead, the throne went to the closest brother. Only if all brothers were dead did the title pass to the next generation. But this arrangement left ample room for ambiguity. It was not uncommon for the princes of the cities to launch into full-scale warfare to claim the title of Grand Prince in Kiev. This was only made worse by the spider's web of noble intermarriage and royal familial relations between the cities.

As such, Vladimir, although a great-great-grandson of Rurik and the prince of Novogorod, the second-most-powerful city in the land, had to fight for his throne. After seven years in exile, he endured a grueling campaign to win Kiev from his brother.

But once in power, Vladimir strengthened the Rus' lands through decisive leadership, securing its borders from nomadic raiders and bringing errant princes to heel. The next order of business: reforming Russian religion.

Most of the early Rus' worshiped a pantheon of pagan gods who were similar in several respects to those of Norse culture. The chief deity, Perun, was god of the sky and lightning, similar to Thor. Veles, like Loki, was god of the underworld and a trickster; Mokosh, like Freya, was a fertility goddess. Druid-like priests performed animistic rituals that followed the seasons and honored the spirits of the natural world through wooden or stone idols. The deep forests surrounding towns were forbidding spiritual places where human power waned and unspoken, primal danger was around each tree.

But by his accession, Vladimir was considering turning from his traditional pagan beliefs and instead adopting one of the great monotheistic world religions he had likely encountered via travelers passing through his lands. His grandmother, Princess Olga (today an Orthodox saint), had already been baptized in Constantinople and persistently encouraged her grandson to follow her lead and convert to Christianity. But Vladimir was cautious, aware of the weight of a decision that could determine Russia's political alliances and unify its people for centuries to come. And so the Grand Prince mustered together his boyars to discuss the possibility of converting his court and the entire Rus' populace. It was not a decision to be made on a whim.

Reaching an impasse with the boyars, Vladimir sent emissaries to the Catholic Germans, Muslim Volga Bulgars, and Orthodox Byzantines. He also received Jewish representatives. The information from these officials would provide him with a menu of religions to pick from. He could evaluate each and make his decision fully informed.

Vladimir dismissed Judaism offhand. The fact that there was no Jewish homeland was evidence that God had forsaken these people, according to Vladimir, and circumcision was hardly an appealing initiation rite. The report on the Bulgars given by Vladimir's agents paralleled ibn Fadlan's: to the diplomats, they seemed disgusting and miserable. Furthermore, Vladimir was wary of the Muslim restrictions on pork and alcohol: in his words, "Drinking is the joy of all the Rus'," so restricting booze would infuriate his subjects. His representatives saw neither joy nor beauty among the stoic Germans, and thus Catholicism could be ruled out as well.

Yet the diplomats sent to Constantinople were awestruck. The Byzantine emperor, Basil II, rolled out the red carpet for Vladimir's delegation.[13] The Rus' were welcomed warmly and given a tour of Constantinople by Basil's inner circle. At a time when Russian cities were tangled, muddy, wood-built collections of huts, filled with livestock wandering grimy roads, it is unsurprising that Constantinople dazzled with its paved streets, running water, and hundreds of thousands of inhabitants who strolled its thoroughfares, worked in its lavish palaces, and watched chariot races in its massive stone hippodrome. Wondrous mechanical birds chirped in the imperial throne room, and the throne itself could rise and tower over visitors. Constantinople's religious heart, the Hagia Sophia – at the time 500 years old but still one of the largest structures on Earth, and topped with the largest dome in the world – opened into a massive space sparkling with precious stones and gilded with glistening gold. The bright interior of the cathedral caught the emissaries off-guard as sun streamed through its high windows and shone off the walls. They were stupefied by its shimmering floor, powerful acoustics, and the divine smell of sweet incense. As a high point of the visit, the emperor invited the diplomats to participate in liturgy.

On their return, the Rus' envoys described the scene to Vladimir poetically:

We knew not whether we were in heaven or on earth. For on earth there is no such splendor or such beauty, and we are at a loss how to describe it. We only know that God dwells there among men, and their service is fairer than the ceremonies of other nations. For we cannot forget that beauty. Every man, after tasting something sweet, is afterward unwilling to accept that which is bitter.[14]

Vladimir was sold, but he had some business to take care of first. A military victory, preferably one that helped the Byzantines, would truly legitimize the conversion. The next year, Vladimir besieged and took the town of Cherson on the Crimean Peninsula, returning the outpost back into Byzantine hands. In exchange, Basil II offered his sister, Anna. Anna was not only close kin to Basil, but *porphyrogenita*: born in the porphyry-lined palace birthing-room, making her a pure-blooded, inside member of Byzantine royalty. Vladimir was happy

---

13. Basil II's actions here go somewhat against his reputation. Known as the "Bulgar Slayer," legend has it that during one successful military campaign into the lands north of Byzantine territory, Basil II blinded 99 out of every 100 captives, leaving the one with a single eye to lead the rest back home.

14. Cross, *Laurentian Text*, 111.

to convert and be baptized, doing so in Crimea just prior to his marriage to Anna in 988. The union meant that the Rurikid and Byzantine royal families were now intertwined.

Was Vladimir's conversion a sincere acceptance of a new confession of faith, or a strategy to gain international friends? Here, again, the exact story is hard to pin down. Scholars might stipulate that Vladimir's conversion, and his choice to convert his entire populace, were due to his desire to gain fruitful allies more than genuine religious interest. And, of course, it is likely that the tale in the chronicles is to some extent polished to make Vladimir out as a pious hero.

Regardless, thanks to Vladimir's leadership, the people of Rus' were baptized into Eastern Orthodox Christianity. This was not always consensual, and was often done in large groups, as even religious art relates. A legend quickly arose that St. Andrew, one of Jesus' original 12 disciples, visited Russia shortly after the Resurrection, and so Andrew became Russia's patron saint.

In adopting Christianity, Russia joined the region's dominant religious community and a tradition with a rich history. But the European church was split. Roman Catholicism and Eastern Orthodoxy were already, at this time, worlds apart. Much of Eastern Orthodoxy drew from the cultures of Greece and the Eastern Mediterranean, whereas Catholicism reflected

Russians are baptized en masse, 988, in an early-20th-century depiction by Klavdiy Leebedev.

its coming-of-age in Rome and Western Europe. Whereas Roman Catholicism emphasized the authority of the head of the church in Rome, Orthodox adherents and priests relied on scripture enriched by the writings of Church Fathers as sources of authority. One of the major theological points of early schism was the nature of the Holy Spirit: Orthodox authorities argued that the Spirit issued from the Father alone, while Catholics held that the Spirit issued both from the Father and Son. In addition, Orthodox thought eschewed the humanism and philosophical analysis Catholicism inherited from Greek and Roman thinkers, leaning instead into the mysterious and awe-inspiring aspects of God. Orthodox teachings emphasized the need for devotion, sacrifice, suffering, and martyrdom.

Thus were created two divergent churches that, while agreeing on many of the most fundamental tenets – for example, Christ's divinity, the virgin birth, and the transubstantiation of the Eucharist into the literal body and blood of Christ – emphasized different aspects of God and fit different cultural contexts. For Russia, this meant that, from the start, there existed a strong monastic culture; for centuries, rather than urban universities or libraries, fortified and self-sustaining religious outposts were the country's beacons of literacy, philosophy, and art. For much of Russian history, the Orthodox Church operated with parallel power to the state, at times even surpassing the power of the tsar. Church power was only legally curtailed in the late 17th century. And today, once more, the Russian Orthodox Church is seeing a resurgence.

Many aspects of Orthodoxy, especially in its Russian expression, make room for a Christianity that can coexist with some superstition. Russians remain notorious for their love of horoscopes and spiritualist dabbling, and traces of early Slavic pagan rituals live on in Russian culture. Some superstitious Russians work to appease their mischievous home spirit, called a *domovoi*, lest it get angry and cause the resident to lose valuable domestic objects like keys. Bathhouses, often dark, foreboding buildings on a country property, are places of levity when used collectively but a cursed place if visiting alone. It is easy to see how the Russian "red corner," a part of a kitchen or living room designated to display a family's Christian icons and candles to bring protection and good fortune, is perhaps a holdover from pagan house altars. The same can not be said for many of the Christians of Western Europe and the U.S., who typically regard such things as antireligious mumbo-jumbo.

Still, the Russian version of Orthodoxy took hold swiftly. It copied Byzantine practice in broad strokes while adapting where necessary. The heavenly Byzantine Hagia Sophia Vladimir's diplomats had raved about received two Russian counterparts much humbler than the original. In 1011, St. Sophia Cathedral in Kiev opened, followed by another St. Sophia Cathedral in Novgorod in 1050. The churches took pride of place in the cities' kremlins, the fortified core of medieval Russian towns that acted like a Greek acropolis or Californian presidio. Yet some architectural sacrifices had to be made in order to fit the needs of the Russian climate. Open-air porticoes had to be closed in, the walls whitewashed for protection, and semicircular domes given their distinctive "onion" curves to allow snow to slough off easily. The final result is the iconic ensemble we know today.

As Kiev is now part of Ukraine, the cathedral in Novgorod is today the oldest church in Russia. Further, while Kiev's cathedral underwent repairs and refurbishment throughout history, Novgorod's cathedral retains much more of the original design and 11th-century character, for good or ill. Even 1500 years after its construction, the Hagia Sophia in Constantinople is still imposing, but St. Sophia in Novgorod today comes off as small, squat, and asymmetrical, a little lopsided no matter what angle you look at it. The interior feels cramped and dim, a far cry from the vaulting, bright cathedrals of much of the Christian world elsewhere.

Yet, to the early medieval Russians, seeing a building of that size, and of stone no less, would have been a divine experience in itself. Entering a cavernous construction housing colorful frescoes, sweet odors, and a reverent atmosphere probably felt like entering a piece of heaven on earth. Still, many common Russians kept practicing their paganism at home, and it took 900 more years to fully shut down pagan habits throughout Russia.

If Vladimir's choice to adopt Orthodox Christianity was informed by a desire to gain allies and enrich his state, he succeeded. By adopting Orthodoxy and cultivating a tight

St. Sophia Cathedral in Novgorod, demonstrating how the early Russians adapted Byzantine architecture to their towns. Image credit: Scaliger (Dreamstime).

relationship with Constantinople, the Rus' joined what some scholars call the "Byzantine commonwealth": a network of peoples stretching from the Balkans and Central Europe into Russia and the Black Sea that all maintained close diplomatic ties to, benefited from economic cooperation with, and drew aspects of their culture from the Byzantine Empire. The Rus' soon adopted the Cyrillic alphabet, which was adapted from Greek specifically for spreading Christianity to Slavic peoples. Russia received increased economic benefits with closer trade ties to one of the wealthiest states in the world, and Rus' visitors to Constantinople became even more common. Rus' and Byzantine nobility intermarried, although it seems Rus' sources exaggerated how often this happened (probably out of pride) and Byzantine sources downplayed their frequency (probably out of shame). Rus' religion followed the lead of officials in Byzantium, with priests and patriarchs regularly making the trek there for official business.[15] One of the most feared units in the Byzantine army, the prestigious Varangian Guard tasked with guarding the emperor, was drawn from young Rus' men, who would serve for a few years in their youth before moving on to continue illustrious careers as professional soldiers and adventurers. Through their close association with Byzantium, the trade, diplomatic, and military influence of the Rus' grew. Kiev and Novgorod became centers of power that welcomed prestigious travelers from around the known world.

The life of the Viking warlord Harald Hadrada demonstrates just how integrated into Christendom Kievan Rus' became following its adoption of Christianity. After losing a battle for the Danish throne in 1030, Harald moved into exile and served first the Grand Prince of Kiev and then in the Varangian Guard of the Byzantine emperor before returning to Rus'. In 1045, he left Novgorod to claim the Norwegian throne, which he did successfully. With the death of England's Edward the Confessor in 1066, Hadrada tried for England as well. He was killed in the Battle of Stamford Bridge by the army of Harold Godwinson, who was himself killed later that year at the Battle of Hastings by the Norman William the Conqueror. As Harald's story shows, the Rus' nation Vladimir formed could act as a hub for travelers, adventurers, and warriors from around the region.

Vladimir has been dubbed "Vladimir the Great" by historians looking back on his rule. His reign saw economic prosperity, international prominence, and political security, but its most significant event was Vladimir's adoption of Christianity, a decision that steered and ultimately defined the nature of Russian civilization.

But as Vladimir aged, his reign showed signs of weakness. His son Sviatopolk, seeing that his father's days were numbered, began assembling an army to oust his father from power and take the Kievan throne for himself. Vladimir discovered the plot and had Sviatopolk thrown in prison. However, shortly before Vladimir's death in 1015, Sviatopolk was released. Disorder exploded into the Rus' lands. Emboldened and intent on revenge, he began systematically removing his brothers from the picture so that there would be no doubt that

---

15. Archaeologists have even discovered Old Slavonic graffiti inside the Hagia Sophia in Constantinople, apparently doodled by a bored Rus' pilgrim.

Sviatopolk would inherit the Rus' lands and be Grand Prince. His pious and quiet younger brothers Boris and Gleb had been his father's favorites; they were murdered in cold blood by Sviatopolk's supporters.

Another brother, Yaroslav, fought back. When Yaroslav emerged the victor of a brutal three-year war, Sviatopolk was sent into exile. Yaroslav was made Grand Prince in 1019. Boris and Gleb were later canonized for dying as holy Orthodox martyrs, meeting their deaths with meekness. Today, Sviatopolk carries the appellation "the Accursed." While the struggle between Sviatopolk and Yaroslav had been especially bloody, it was not atypical of the dynastic jostling that occurred each time the Grand Prince died.

Kievan Rus' reached its zenith under Yaroslav, who ruled as Grand Prince from 1019 to 1054. Yaroslav is known as "the Wise," a nickname granted to him for establishing a library in Novgorod and encouraging arts and education in the Rus' lands. He also codified the disparate laws of the realm, greatly expanding the efficacy of his government, in what became known as the *Russkaya Pravda* ("Russian Truth/Rights"), Russia's first legal code. Further, the Rus' defended themselves from the Polovtsians, nomads from the southeast, and expanded to fill the territory between the Baltic and Black Seas. All of these actions maintained the Rus' position as a prosperous center of trade. The rule of Yaroslav was, by many measures, a golden age of early Russian civilization.

But again, the succession question threatened to undo all that Yaroslav and Vladimir had worked to accomplish. Yaroslav's golden age persisted only until his great-grandson, Vladimir II Monomakh, died in 1125. Monomakh boasted a Byzantine royal pedigree on his mother's side. While this legitimized his rule, it was not enough to maintain order on his death. Local factions and rival branches of the Rurikids had gained enough control that the final decision of who should succeed him was in the air. This time, there was no decisive winner in the fratricidal struggle. Rus' splintered around Vladimir's extended family.

For more than a century, the lands of Russia were divided into multiple self-governing cities. More than a dozen settlements were effectively miniature states of their own, though they remained unified in culture and language. Among the most prominent were Novgorod, the ancient merchant city in the north; Vladimir, often joined with neighboring Suzdal, to the northeast; Smolensk and Chernigov, in the center; Pereyaslavl, in the southeast; and Kiev, further south. While the Grand Prince remained the nominal ruler over all the cities, as it had been since the time of Rurik's sons, the title became much more ceremonial than an indicator of true political power as Rus' decentralized.

With the death of Vladimir II Monomakh and the lack of an heir that might tie the Rus' together once more, each city-state was ruled by their own branch of the Rurikid dynasty or local nobles. Complex alliances and roiling wars between the cities were common. Subjugated cities showed their subservience by paying tribute in the form of money or manpower to other cities, creating patronage networks that could change swiftly with rises in power and shifts in diplomacy.

These independent polities could by turns be embroiled in brutal war or welcome close relations with each other. Outright conquest was rare, but one city might extract tribute in the form of trade goods or gold from another, making it a vassal bound to loyalty and service. Add to this landscape diplomatic marriages and networks of tribute, and there soon arose a dense and intricate web of interaction that could either empower or humiliate.

Without a strong leader in Kiev, though, one city took a radical and exceptional turn: Novgorod, that ancient trade hub on the Volkhov where Rurik first came ashore. Its story stands in contrast to the autocratic leadership wielded by the likes of Vladimir and Yaroslav and bucks our typical expectations of medieval Russia.

Around the time Rurik had arrived, the people of Novgorod seem to have moved their city from a small lakeside island to the river mouth. The island, today called "Rurik's Stronghold" ("*Rurikovo Gorodishche*"), is likely the one ibn Fadlan heard tales of among the Bulgars, although it is much smaller than the rumor implies. The name "Novgorod" is itself a portmanteau of two words meaning "New City" (*Novy Gorod*),[16] implying that the main settlement today is distinct from another older one nearby. Novgorod straddled the river: on one bank sat the imposing kremlin, with its gold-domed cathedral and sprawling palaces. On the other was the market square, dominated by a skyline of church towers above bustling market tents. Between them, the sluggish Volkhov, the artery of the city, was spanned by a wooden bridge. The river was busy with trade boats in warm months and sledges when the water froze. The market was the draw for many, just off the main road through town, and attracted merchants hawking wares from around the known world. It was perhaps the most cosmopolitan city of the Rurikovichi.

During the time of a unified Kievan Rus', Novgorod had been the second city of the Grand Princedom. It was traditionally where the prince next in line to the throne was stationed before the ruling Grand Prince passed away. It was here that Grand Princes Vladimir and Yaroslav had first cut their teeth in the political arena, gaining experience before taking control of the full panoply of Rus' cities.

Perhaps it was Novgorod's mercantile streak that fostered a class of free traders with a culture that was wary of all-powerful rulers. Maybe it was a longstanding informal arrangement that dated back into time immemorial; after all, it was the city's populace, and their representatives, who had first invited Rurik and his family to settle down. Regardless, by the time the Rus' cities diverged, city government had evolved into a sophisticated and unique system of civic engagement.

Novgorod's true republican period can be traced to 1136, not long after the Rus' cities drifted apart on the death of Vladimir II Monomakh. The city's prince was sent packing, fleeing an angry mob. This set the precedent that Rus' princes were only allowed to rule by the grace of the citizenry; after all, the argument went, if citizens can expel rulers, surely they

---

16. Note the similarity between the Russian word for city, *gorod*, and the Norse word *gard* meaning "enclosed place," which is often used in placenames. This is another clue to Russia's Scandinavian heritage.

A veche meeting in winter as painted by Vasily Khudyakov, 1861.

can invite them, too. Thus, being a prince was to be an invite-only opportunity for the royal Rurikovich families of neighboring cities. The city whose prince was chosen to rule over Novgorod gained de facto control over one of the wealthiest cities in Eastern Europe, but was forced to preserve specific privileges for the Novgorodian public in order to remain in power.

The prince's role was markedly more limited than typical medieval rulers'. He could wage war and lead on the battlefield, oversee international relations, and implement laws. Anything more than that and he was liable to find himself facing the unfriendly end of a pitchfork. Various citizen-led councils did most of the grunt work of the government. While we are unsure exactly how they functioned, we know that the elected mayoral office (*posadnik*), nobles, and neighborhood representative-administrators (*tysiatskie*, from the Russian word meaning "thousand") collaboratively decided and implemented policy for Novgorodian locals. These administrators, along with church officials, were tasked with day-to-day governance. They all were overseen by the chief executive: the prince.[17]

---

17. See Sevanstyanova, "In Quest of the Key Democratic Institution of Medieval Rus,'" and Paul, "Was The Prince of Novgorod a 'Third-Rate Bureaucrat' after 1136?"

To tackle wide-impact questions, citizens gathered to discuss policy in an open council, called a *veche*.[18] When the *veche*'s bell was rung, all free men could convene in the large trading square along the river to discuss issues facing the city and vote on the solution. *Veche* meetings could turn disorderly, chaotic, and loud. But the *veche* is evidence that, as remarkable as it may seem to us today, Russia has a robust democratic tradition dating back nearly a millennium. While, admittedly, it is hard to pinpoint the details, and we have no evidence of any kind of constitution or legal system that might have maintained liberal traditions, autocracy is perhaps not as inseparable from the Russian cultural heritage as one might think.

Still, Novgorod abided by the same spiritual culture as the rest of the Rus' cities, and it was not immune to the inter-city intrigue pervasive in Russia at the time. Perhaps no tale demonstrates how deeply the Rus' were impacted by Vladimir's adoption of Orthodoxy and its impact on their worldview than that of the icon of Our Lady of the Sign, which has since passed into legend.[19] As always, the details have likely been embellished in the retelling, but the excitement of the story remains.

It goes something like this:

In 1170, four of the Russian principalities, Vladimir-Suzdal, Smolensk, Murom, and Polotsk, created a coalition against Novgorod. What started as a minor spat over tribute ballooned into all-out war.

The conflict was looking bleak for the Republic. Novgorod was besieged. Its inhabitants scuttled about quietly, anxiously awaiting the day when their enemies' forces would burst in and destroy the city, pillage its populace, or enforce a harsh peace. Novgorod was sharply outnumbered. The situation seemed hopeless.

Archbishop Ivan, the city's religious leader, was praying quietly in one of Novgorod's ancient cathedrals. Suddenly, he heard a voice telling him to take the holy icon of Our Lady of the Sign, a portrayal of the Virgin Mary praying while pregnant with Jesus, from its normal place in a church near the market square and display it brazenly on the ramparts to the enemy armies on the other side of town. The icon was a fixture in the city, a holy symbol of God's protection, and removing it from its sacred place could expose it to desecration. But Ivan obeyed nonetheless.

Ivan processed across Novgorod, icon in hand, marching boldly with a band of religious brethren. He crossed over the Volkhov River bridge at the heart of the city. He passed through the kremlin, where, no doubt, troops were mustering to prepare a final heroic defense of the city. He wove through the streets of Novgorod's oldest quarters, where citizens darted, stashing valuables and preparing for battle. Finally, he reached the ramparts and climbed to the top, peeking over at a massive enemy formation.

---

18. There is some debate over whether the *veche* was a uniquely Novgorodian institution or whether it was practiced more widely in Russia. Pskov, not far from Novgorod, also had a *veche*, but scholars are not sure how closely it resembled Novgorod's. There is some evidence that *veches* existed elsewhere, but little is conclusive.

19. See "Skazanie o bitve Novgorodtsev s Suzdal'tsami."

No sooner had he placed the icon on the wall, facing the besiegers, than a skirmish began. Missiles flew from the enemy formations, and an arrow struck the icon just below the eye. In a righteous fury, Ivan twirled the icon around. He noticed a miraculous tear streaming down the Virgin Mary's face from where the arrow had embedded itself in the wood.

Soon the attack fizzled out, and the attackers returned to their line. That night, terror gripped the enemy camp. The next morning, the Novgorodian forces left the protection of their walls and counterattacked. They handily drove off their rivals, chasing them from the walls. Novgorod was saved, with God's help and the help of the icon of Our Lady of the Sign.

A new Novgorodian icon was produced to commemorate the event. Like a comic strip, it shows in three scenes the story of the icon being transported across the river to the other

The story of Our Lady of the Sign, told in an icon.

side of town, then an arrow hitting the icon, and then the heroic counterattack. Visitors to Novgorod today can see the icon of Our Lady of the Sign, the one used in battle, complete with arrow-hole, in the old St. Sophia Cathedral in the center of the city. It is still venerated by many locals. Some more adventurous travelers can even locate the place where the miracle is supposed to have taken place, marked by an abandoned monastery just inside the crumbled remains of the city's walls.

The Battle of Novgorod and its miraculous salvation demonstrate that Kievan Rus', as forged by grand princes like Vladimir and Yaroslav, was a mystical, religious world of warfare and politics, where battles between fellow cities could be decided by intense prayer, beautiful holy objects, and God's shifting favor. Not even princes were exempt; if anything was to be learned from Vladimir's rise and Sviatopolk's bloody ambition, it was that the right would always triumph, through God's justice.

AS ALIEN AS medieval Russia may seem today, this lost world was the foundation on which later Russia built, ideologically, culturally, and philosophically. It may be a dim past, far removed, yet its head continues to rear.

Any medieval Russian city, even a confederation of four, was nothing compared to the foe the principalities were about to face. The Byzantine-inspired, Orthodox world of pre-Mongol Rus', one of prayer and art, quasi-democracy and trade riches, war and desperation, was about to face an existential threat, one that would have wide-ranging implications for centuries to come.

3

SUBJUGATION: RUS' AND TATAR TRIBUTE

Meet the Mongols | The defense of Rus' | Novgorod writes | A shift to Moscow | A yoke broken, a nation forged

The Mongol invasion was hailed thus:

> *For our sins, unknown nations arrived. No one knew their origin or whence they came, or what religion they practiced. That is known only to God, and perhaps to wise men learned in books.*[20]

Faced with the greatest force the medieval world could encounter, the Rus' were confounded, frustrated, hopeless, terrified, confused. Given the medieval Russian conception of the world, it is unsurprising that they interpreted the Mongol invasion as judgment from God. It must have seemed like the world was ending, spiraling out of control. The only recourse would be to pray for mercy and repent. And hope for a miracle.

Raiders from the steppes were nothing new. Throughout its history, Kievan Rus' faced the perennial problem of stopping mounted incursions into its lands. But the Mongol invasion was unprecedented in its scale and ambition. Here was a vast horde, nearly invincible, that did not just want one year's harvest or a bundle of trade goods. The Mongols wanted domination.

The Mongol invasion was a radical break in the development of the Rus'. But not all the consequences were negative; instead, Russia found itself both enriched and imbued with new purpose after freeing itself from the Tatar yoke.

BY THE TIME they came into contact with the cities of the Rus', the Mongols were already hardened veterans with an empire at their backs. The Mongol people (referred to by Russians as "Tatars") were natives of what are today parts of modern Mongolia, Russia, and northern China. Their homeland was high, dry, and harsh, hardly the environment that would foster a world-spanning empire.

But, raised in a culture steeped in horse-archery, herding, and nomadism, Mongol warriors were superbly effective. Almost everything in Mongol life prepared them for constant

---

20. Zenkovsky, *Medieval Russia's Epics, Chronicles, and Tales*, 59.

movement, and these skills translated perfectly into extended military campaigns. The Mongols' nomadic society taught them to travel with flocks of animals and forage off the land indefinitely, practices their rivals never needed to refine. Their ability to strike hard and fast on horseback, cover great distances quickly, and soundly defeat slow, infantry-heavy forces of the time made Mongol tactics the stuff of legend.

The early years of the man who bound the rival Mongol tribes together and made them a formidable conquering force, Genghis Khan, are shrouded in mystery. He came from a leading family of the clans of the steppe, with noble blood from his parents. His birth and rise to power were hailed with powerful omens and optimistic portents. In his twenties, he emerged as the leader of a united confederation of tribes from the north of China. From there, he cast his sights further afield. The Mongol people, led by hundreds of thousands of mounted warriors, exploded out of the steppe, a tide sweeping across Eurasia.

Most of China and Persia were taken by 1220, and the Mongol war machine only gained momentum. As more land was conquered, more trade was funneled through Mongol hands, more tribute riches could be leveraged into strengthening the army, and more manpower and expertise could reinforce the Mongols' already formidable force. This flexibility and determination created a force that seemed unstoppable.

While the Mongols were strongest in open territory like their home steppes, where they could use horse archers to their advantage and could live off the land indefinitely, their siege tactics, gleaned from Chinese captives, were also ingenious. At the siege of one Central Asian city in 1209, the Mongols diverted a river to thirst out the populace. The tactic worked, but the diverted river also flooded the Mongols' own camp.

All these aspects combined to make the Mongols a terrifying force to face, one that Rus' was not equipped to answer.

In 1223, the Mongols were consolidating their hold on Asia and beginning to move into Europe. Genghis Khan dispatched some of his top officers from Persia with a small army to scout out lands to the northwest for future conquest. Covering roughly the same route as ibn Fadlan had taken 300 years earlier, winding through high mountains and down onto the southern plains, the Mongol force crossed into Rus'. In response, the Kievan prince, leading allies from a handful of other Rus' cities, rushed to meet the invaders. After a clash, the Mongol force began to retreat, and the Rus' pursued. After several days, the prince's forces were stretched out and exhausted, but hopeful that they could deal a decisive blow to turn back the invaders.

It was at this point the Mongols turned their mounts and counterattacked. The Kievan prince was soundly defeated, with some estimates putting Russian losses at 90 percent. But the Mongols did not press their advantage and push back into Rus' territory. This was merely a scouting party, and, their mission accomplished, they returned to their homeland. Presumably, the Russians were both relieved and perplexed that the Mongols had cut their attack short. They were probably more than a little afraid, too, that they might return. But, for the time being, it seemed like just another nomadic incursion. A deadly annoyance, but little more.

When the Mongols, under the command of Genghis's successor, Batu Khan, returned in 1237, they arrived with the intention of complete conquest and the incorporation of the Rus' cities into their sprawling empire. The ancient towns of Vladimir and Ryazan were the first to fall. In 1238 and 1239, the Mongols took the Crimean Peninsula. Finally, the crucial city of Kiev was taken in 1240, effectively ending its dominance over the rest of Rus' and disbanding the political systems of the Grand Prince.

The Mongols seize Vladimir. Sixteenth-century illustration.

The campaign lasted just three years. The Rus' cities had no time to defend themselves, much less organize a coordinated resistance. And they had hardly stood a chance as the Mongol forces, bolstered by tens of thousands of experienced troops from throughout Eurasia, gathered outside city walls. Archaeological evidence, like skeletons of civilians found crushed under rubble or huddling in makeshift bunkers, testify to the terror that gripped the common people. Rumors of these gruesome scenes likely terrified residents of neighboring cities. Some chose to surrender rather than face destruction.

After taking Russia and ensuring its subjugation, the Mongols moved on to Eastern Europe, adding Hungary and the Danube River basin to their holdings.

By 1260, the Mongol Empire had reached its height. It included much of Korea and China, the entirety of Central Eurasia, Persia, the Middle East, swathes of Europe, and the majority of Russia. However, keeping control of all these disparate lands under the person of the khan presented challenges. Succession disputes arose between the descendants of Genghis, each with a claim to all the Mongol hordes. The disputes were settled by dividing up the land into four parts: the Ilkhanate, centered in Persia; the Yuan Dynasty, taking up most of China under the leadership of Kublai Khan; the Chagatai Khanate, nominally superior to the others and containing much of central Asia and the Mongolian heartland; and the Golden Horde, which encompassed Russia, the north Caucasus, and southern Siberia.

The Golden Horde, the Rus' cities' new overlord, was ruled by a Tatar court in the new capital of Sarai, along the Volga and near the Caspian Sea. Like most settlements in the area, Sarai arose to take advantage of commerce: it occupied a point on the river where trade routes from Persia and China, crossing the Caspian by ship, intersected with the river routes into the Russian interior and on to the Mediterranean or Baltic. Russia was now part of a system of government, exchange, and communication that stretched over mind-boggling distances, from the Sea of Japan to the Pannonian plain.

Administering such large swathes of land would be a challenge even today, much less in a time when the fastest means of communication was via horse. But the Mongols' innovations in bureaucracy helped alleviate this problem. Subjugated territories – in Russia's case, its cities – were given a high degree of independence as long as they paid regular tribute to the khan, swearing their subordination and providing human, material, and monetary support. Princes who resisted might be killed, with more pliant nobles instituted in their place. Those who surrendered quickly usually escaped with their lives and their city, and maybe even with their position.

In Russia, the Mongols empowered the princes of the town of Vladimir, which had been quick to welcome the Mongols rather than fight them, to rule the Russian lands as the Mongols' representatives. The prince of Vladimir was now given the title of Grand Prince, in the Kievan tradition, with the full backing of the invincible Mongol hordes. The Khan sent trained bureaucrats to work with the Grand Princes of Vladimir to assess and collect tribute from the other Rus' cities. This tribute was usually collected from each family in the form of goods like furs, grain, honey, or other products. Sources are too vague to determine exactly how dear the tribute was, so it is difficult to say whether it was an undue burden or not.

With Vladimir's supremacy, the inter-city feuding had to end; thus, paradoxically, the Mongol invasion ushered in a time of internal peace. So long as Russian cities did not rock the boat and kept the tribute flowing, they could expect peace and prosperity and the freedom to maintain their local culture and customs. Russia's relative backwardness likely helped: while wealthy Persia and China enticed Mongol rulers to settle in and integrate with the locals, in Russia, they kept their distance. It seems that there simply was not enough to draw long-term migration. Better instead for bureaucrats to stop by every now and again and get their dole. While Rus' rulers were put under supervision, and they found themselves at the behest of the court in Sarai, Russian Orthodox religion, Byzantine culture, and riverine commerce continued, and in many cases even flourished.

One city escaped integration into the Mongol system: Novgorod. The merchant republic instead enjoyed a golden age brought on by Mongol hegemony. To this day, the common narrative in Russian history remains that Novgorod outright defied the Mongol invasion and clung to independence as the last Rus' holdout. At the center of this tale is the mythic figure of Prince Alexander Nevsky, whose life has since passed into legend.

The story goes that, in 1236, just as southern Russia was coming under Mongol rule, Alexander humbly took up residence as prince of Novgorod after being duly invited from his native Vladimir. He was a young member of the Rurikid line, ambitious, just, and eager to prove himself. He soon got his chance: when Swedish invaders came ashore in Novgorodian territory on the River Neva, Alexander led a counterattack and routed them. From this victory, he earned both the nickname "Nevsky" ("of the Neva") and the adoration of the Novgorodian people.

Time passed, during which Alexander ruled with wisdom and fairness. When the Tatars appeared in Novgorod demanding tribute, he rebuked them, retaining Novgorod's cherished independence. Then, he turned his attention to the West, where Catholic German knights of the Teutonic Order had begun a crusade against the Orthodox Russians, plundering and attacking the peaceful, unarmed populace in an effort to convert them to their branch of Christianity. Novgorod was under attack, its independence at stake, the survival of the *veche* in the balance.

Alexander led a desperate stand, intercepting the invaders west of the city. Nevsky feigned a retreat onto the surface of a frozen lake in early spring. The Germans followed, sensing an easy victory. At that crucial point, the lightly-clad Russians struck back, surrounding the Catholics. Many of the Germans, clad in heavy Western-style plate armor, drowned in the frigid waters. The Novgorodians were victorious and free to fight another day. Their republic lived on.

Nevsky thus entered the popular imagination as a national hero. He represents an unflagging early defender of the Russian fatherland from greedy, unscrupulous, ruthless

Novgorodian prince Alexander Nevsky, center with raised sword, drives off the Teutonic invaders in a mosaic in a St. Petersburg metro station near the site of his victory on the Neva. Image credit: Gutaper (Dreamstime).

Western invaders, able to rally the people into a defense that was both effective and played to the Russian people's strengths.

This is a great tale, and one that even Russia's leaders usually endorse as true. Yet it may be far from what really happened. In 1938, a movie was made based on Nevsky's exploits, and it has since then heavily influenced the public imagination. Today it is nearly impossible to untangle what is accepted fact from what was added by a Stalin-era film crew. In short, the story is a patchwork. Like so much else from the Mongol period, the real episode was much more convoluted and nuanced.[21]

First, Novgorod did not so much defy the Mongol yoke as merely escape it. No one is certain why the Tatar invaders overlooked the wealthy trade center of the Rus'. It seems that the Mongols were happy to take all the lands to the south and east of Novgorod, but stopped short of taking the republic. It could be that the terrain was inhospitable: boggy, forested land and cold weather were conducive neither to cavalry attacks nor protracted sieges. In addition, in the wet seasons of spring and fall, Russia's lowlands of rich, clay-filled soil turn to *rasputitsa*, a viscous slop that could swallow people, horses, and wagons and make maneuvering impossible.

---

21. Halperin, *Russia and the Golden Horde*, is a fantastic resource on the Rus', and Novgorod, during the time of the Mongol occupation.

Still, the fact remains that Novgorod did answer to Mongol authority. The *veche* continued, but Novgorodian emissaries dealt with Vladimir and Sarai when it came to international relations, tribute payments, and commercial charters. It seems that an uneasy détente existed between Novgorod and the Tatars.

As for Nevsky himself, he was not exactly a hero of resistance. The prince was a boyar of the royal family of Vladimir, the khan's appointed patsies for ensuring the Rus' cities stayed firmly in line. He ruled Novgorod merely as one part of his rotation between Vladimir, Novgorod, and Kiev. More likely he was a candidate chosen by Vladimirian rulers with the approval of Tatar overseers, then rubber-stamped by Novgorod's civic officials. The battle against the Swedes for which Nevsky earned his epithet is also hard to confirm.

Moreover, while the Teutonic Knights were a real German religious order sent to crusade among the Lithuanians[22] and Russians, we have very little evidence of what came to be called the "Battle on the Ice." Chronicles of the time mention a battle only in passing, and it is only later histories that added the juicy details. Its location, for one, is hard to pin down. Tradition holds that the clash occurred somewhere on Lake Peipus, west of Novgorod, but so far, no significant archaeological finds, like the medieval armor and swords one might expect from an aquatic battlefield, have emerged from its silty bottom. The Battle on the Ice probably did happen, but it may have been much less of the epic set-piece that we imagine.[23]

Nevsky's other actions are less those of a defiant renegade and more those of a calculated politician. In one tale from the chronicles, he personally escorted a pair of Mongol agents through Novgorod to protect them from citizens' ire as they inspected the city to calculate tribute, which was paid to Vladimir, and thence passed along to Sarai. In a final irony, Nevsky died in 1261 while returning from one of his many trips to pay homage to the khan in Sarai.

Regardless of the particulars, Novgorod flourished in the Mongol era. With trade routes secure thanks to Mongol occupation, and disputes with neighboring cities brokered by Mongol officials, Novgorodian and foreign merchants were free to take advantage of safe transit within Russia and beyond. Novgorod became the eastern terminus of the Hanseatic League, stretching its economic tendrils all the way to mercantile cities of eastern England. Foreigner quarters sprang up near the trade square to house merchants from afar, each sporting its own churches, as Greek, Norse, German, Middle Eastern, and even Western European traders came to Novgorod to make their fortunes.

Archaeological evidence further confirms that this was Novgorod's high point. Both church construction and icon painting exploded, indicating high levels of patronage by wealthy local merchants who were likely also involved in the *veche*. And thousands of artifacts of day-to-day life have also been discovered around the city. Novgorod's uniquely rich, low-oxygen soil preserved many workaday tools constructed from organic material, including

---

22. While Rus' was Orthodox at this time, Lithuania was pagan. The nation finally adopted Catholicism in 1368.

23. See Hellie, "Alexander Nevskii's April 5, 1242 Battle on the Ice."

buckets, hollowed logs used as sewers, and entire streets paved and re-paved with layers of planks. From these finds, scholars paint a picture of a thriving Novgorodian citizenry that was capable of funding and completing clever public works using plentiful local lumber. This in contrast to other Russian cities of the time that survived the Mongol invasion but did not flourish. Some, like Kiev, took centuries to recover.

By far the greatest treasures of Novgorodian archaeology, though, are birchbark manuscripts. It was a practice of medieval Novgorodians to peel off the thin bark of the birch trees that grow everywhere in local swamps and scratch into its soft undersides with metal styluses. These manuscripts are not formal histories or stodgy declarations. Rather, they are grocery lists, receipts for jewelry repair, complaints, love letters, reminders – the medieval version of sticky notes, written by people from all kinds of backgrounds. We even have the notebook of a schoolchild, Onfim, whose lessons are interspersed with fanciful childhood doodles of abstract shapes, horsemen, and dragons. The birchbark manuscripts are almost like time travel.[24]

The sheer number of documents found, along with their varied content that implies a diverse authorship, has led scholars to theorize that as much as 90 percent of Novgorod's population may have been literate. Even conservative estimates propose a majority of the population knowing how to read and write, a remarkable feat for the 13th and 14th centuries. This was in part thanks to the library founded by Yaroslav the Wise but undoubtedly encouraged by favorable circumstances created by the Tatar yoke.

ABOUT THE SAME time as the schoolboy Onfim was learning to write, a new city was beginning to flourish. The prince of Vladimir-Suzdal had in 1147 established a trading post on a little rise at a forested river bend. For years, it was small and unremarkable, supervised by minor Rurikids to project Vladimirian economic control. But, in 1304, a succession crisis caused a breakup of the Vladimirian lands. The outpost, named for the river it sat along, Moscow, became the new center for the Vladimirian royal family, through which the Mongols could administer their Rus' holdings.

The new town worked closely with the Tatars to ensure the Rus' cities remained subservient. In return, Moscow received concessions of low tribute, defense subsidies, and the khan's favor. Moscow quickly grew in size and power. Soon, it had become the most powerful settlement in the region.

At the same time, Mongol power started to wane. By 1380, the Rus' cities had begun to chafe under the demands for Mongol tribute. The Black Death had killed thousands, gutted international trade, and made manpower and tribute more difficult to collect. It became clear that a new Tatar campaign was needed to put the Rus' cities back in their place under the Golden Horde.

---

24. These manuscripts are collected and free to be seen (and read) at http://gramoty.ru/birchbark. Many are housed in museums around Russia, including in the history museum of Novgorod's kremlin.

The chief Mongol warlord, Mamai, mustered an army and began to move into Rus' territories, intent on consolidating power once again. The khan himself traveled with Mamai. Meanwhile, the prince of Moscow, Dmitri, sensed an opportunity. He called together a confederation to beat back this Mongol incursion. Dmitri rode at the head of an army made up of troops and nobles from throughout the Rus' lands. According to the account of the campaign, the *Zadonshchina*, Novgorodian forces stayed home.

On September 8, 1380, the sides clashed on the banks of the Don River near modern Tula in a clearing known as Kulikovo Field. It was a fierce and bloody battle, but Dmitri and the Russians prevailed. The khan of the Golden Horde lay dead on the battlefield. Mamai and the Mongols were routed and trudged back to Sarai. Dmitri gained a new epithet: Donskoy, or "of the Don," a reference to his victory.

The Battle of Kulikovo Field was not the death knell for the Tatar Yoke, but it was the beginning of the end. In the years that followed, infighting among the Tatar rulers further undermined the power of the Golden Horde, and the Rus' cities began to circumvent the tribute system or avoid it altogether. Tatar officials, sensing their powerlessness, quit stopping by to collect tribute.

A hundred years later, another Moscow-led force gathered to repulse a new Mongol incursion after the Grand Prince of Moscow refused to pay tribute. Both sides assembled on the banks of the Ugra River, but neither crossed. Instead, for six weeks in the fall of 1480, the armies eyed each other warily across the water. Finally, the Mongol force withdrew without a fight. As the Mongols refused to force a confrontation, the Russian forces were the de facto victors. The Stand on the Ugra River can be considered the true end of the Mongol occupation.

But some pockets of Tatar power remained. In fact, Mongol rump states continued to exist in the city of Kazan (until 1552) and the Crimean Peninsula (until 1783). It took Catherine the Great, in the 18th century, to finally grind out the last vestiges of Mongol power, by then a shadow of its former glory.

WITH THE MONGOLS ousted, the Principality of Muscovy, centered in Moscow, became the preeminent Russian city. This upstart settlement, initially endowed with power by the Mongols, became the Tatars' undoing by leveraging its privileges towards resistance. By first embracing, and then casting off, Mongol subjugation, Moscow found itself positioned to lead the Rus'.

More importantly, though, the Rus' had found a new identity. Emerging from Mongol domination, Russia was not Mongolified; instead, it had created a culture that celebrated the expulsion of pagan invaders. The narrative that Russia had simply thrown off an undue imposed burden through sheer force of will and zealous defense was much simpler than the truth, and also much more compelling.

Both Alexander Nevsky and Dmitri Donskoy were later canonized as Orthodox saints for their stunning holy victories, historical nuance be damned. Nevsky is venerated at a monastery bearing his name, which was created in St. Petersburg in the early 1700s. He remains interred there to this day, the centerpiece of cemeteries containing some of Russia's greatest musicians, philosophers, and statesmen. Dmitri Donskoy today lies at the very heart of Russian power, entombed in the Archangel Cathedral of the Moscow Kremlin.

Far from breaking the Russian spirit, the Mongol subjugation crystallized a new identity: one that was intrinsically Orthodox and fiercely militant, and that emphasized the need for defense against foreign invaders to preserve the fatherland at any cost.

4

SANCTIFICATION AND CENTRALIZATION: MUSCOVITE SUPREMACY AND THE TIME OF TROUBLES

*Moscow among Rus' | Becoming Byzantine
 | Ivans great and terrible | Dmitri, Dmitri, Dmitri*

The Byzantine Empire was dead.

After decades of territorial losses, the empire had shrunk to a fragile shadow of its former greatness. Once the final assault began, Constantinople held on until the very last moment as best it could. A sharply outnumbered coalition of militia, troops, mercenaries, and adventurers from around the Mediterranean manned the walls in a desperate defense. But after 55 days, on May 29, 1453, the wellspring of Orthodox Christianity, the last holdout of the Romans, was conquered by the Muslim Ottoman Turks, who had employed constant artillery fire and brilliant siege engineering to bring down the city. The last emperor died a martyr, fighting in the streets; so chaotic was the battle that his body was never recovered. The gutters ran with blood, and smoke curled over the ancient dome of the Hagia Sophia. The Ottoman sultan entered in triumph.

The Orthodox world shuddered. Where, now, would Byzantium's sacred mantle fall? Who would take its place as the beacon of true Christianity, to hold off the pagan invaders, to embody the continuing spirit of Rome? What great civilization would embrace this rich heritage?

The unlikely answer was found in a muddy trading outpost on the Moscow River. This river town not only took up where Byzantium left off; it cultivated an exceptional sacred autocracy that complemented a religious mission to preserve holy Orthodoxy at all costs. In the centuries following the end of Mongol rule, a strong conception of Russian statehood formed, centered around a powerful royal.

WIELDING THE POWER bestowed upon it by years of Mongol favoritism and intercity coalition-building, Moscow's princes looked to expand. It was time to unify the Rus' lands, fractured and disparate after more than two centuries under the Mongols, into a single entity. With Mongol power dissolved, Moscow was ready to pounce.

Reunifying the Rus' was chiefly the project of Ivan III, who was crowned Grand Prince of Moscow in 1462. Ivan saw the other Rus' cities, the lands once controlled by the first Rurikids, as his rightful inheritance. And, touting a message of Russian independence, Ivan III cultivated many supporters among the nobility who would help him achieve his vision.

A quick succession of campaigns and diplomatic dealings led to the rapid-fire addition of other Rus' cities to the Muscovite lands. In 1471, with support from vassals and allies, Yaroslavl fell; Perm followed in 1472, Rostov in 1473, Tver in 1485, and Viatka in 1489. Soon, Muscovite power stretched throughout central Russia, stretching eastwards towards Siberia. The loose Moscow-led coalition that had pushed back the Mongols at Kulikovo Field and the Ugra River was now a country in its own right.

Unsurprisingly, however, Novgorod was hesitant to join Ivan III's new nation.

Novgorod's citizens were undoubtedly concerned with preserving their city's dearly-held independence and civic culture. They had enjoyed their ancient and special privileges even during Mongol hegemony, negotiating with the other Rus' cities and their Mongol overlords for their preservation. Novgorod would not concede them in the face of an upstart. But how to counter the growing power of Moscow? Novgorod was a trade city, not a military powerhouse. It was a lucrative target ripe for the taking.

A potential solution arose out of Novgorod's semi-democratic institutions: a woman, Marfa Boretskaya. She was the wife of a boyar nobleman and landowner who was heavily involved in city politics. When her husband died, Marfa became one of the wealthiest and most influential people in the city. Not willing to see her beloved Novgorod brought under Muscovite control and with no help forthcoming from the other Rus' cities, she sought aid abroad. Boretskaya conducted desperate negotiations with the Polish-Lithuanian Commonwealth, floating the possibility of Novogorodian vassalage in return for keeping its traditional rights.

A treaty was drafted, but talks were interrupted by Muscovite forces, which arrived at the city gates in 1478. The city fell after a short siege, and the Muscovites destroyed the *veche* square, carting off its bell. Boretskaya was sent into exile. Novgorod was absorbed into the monarchical rule of Moscow, and its time as an independent state ended. The *veche* never convened again.

By the early 1500s, in one prince's reign, Muscovy had spread to cover almost all of European Russia. The major Rus' cities were gathered under Ivan III's rule, the sprawling Rurikid inheritance consolidated into one man. But Ivan had an even greater concern than amassing a kingdom: his legacy.

Ivan III's marriage proved to be just as crucial to Russian history as were his military conquests, perhaps more so. The union was a continuation, a renewal, of the relationship between Constantinople and the Rus' that dated back to Vladimir I's baptism. Of course, Russian culture and faith continued to draw on the Byzantine roots first laid down through trade and then solidified through religious brotherhood. However, in the intervening years, with the Mongol invasion rupturing Eastern Europe but leaving the Byzantines largely unscathed, the two nations had diverged. Now, though, with pre-Ottoman Byzantium no more than a fading dream, Ivan, the ruler of the most powerful remaining Orthodox state, felt he could legitimately lay claim to the Byzantine heritage.

Ironically, the arrangement was proposed by the Vatican. Pope Paul II saw a marriage between Sophia Palaiologina, an exiled niece of the last Byzantine emperor, and Ivan III as an opportunity to bring Russia into the Catholic fold. Ivan agreed enthusiastically; with his territory growing, marrying into the Byzantine imperial family would further legitimize his regal supremacy. The wedding was held in June 1472 in St. Peter's Basilica with full Latin rites. Ivan was unable to be there in person and so arranged a stand-in.

From Rome, Sophia was shipped off to Moscow, where she promptly dropped any pretensions of Catholicism and instead embraced her family's ancestral Orthodoxy. While there is no doubt she was sorely disappointed by the muddy streets and relative poverty of Moscow, she quickly embraced her new homeland. When she died years later, Sophia was buried with honors among the most prestigious Muscovite rulers in the Moscow Kremlin, the gleaming fortress-palace complex overlooking the Moscow River that now served as the beating heart of Ivan's government.

Thanks to this union, all of Ivan's children, through Sophia, would be able to claim direct royal Byzantine blood. Anna, Vladimir I's wife, was long dead, and her family had long since fallen out of power in Constantinople. But no one could replace the final emperors of the empire; they would be royal forever. It was a masterstroke of royal propaganda to reunite the royal houses of Russia and the Byzantines.

After his wedding to Sophia, Ivan meticulously cultivated the notion that Muscovy was the "Third Rome": the first, Rome itself, had fallen in 476, the second, Constantinople, was overrun in 1453, but the third? The third would be immortal. To solidify the connection, Ivan adopted as his royal insignia the double-headed eagle, the heraldic animal of Sophia's family and a symbol of holy dominion dating back millennia. Ivan also dropped the title of "grand prince" and began using "tsar," from the word "caesar," with all the attendant imperial connotations he could now borrow from Rome, via Byzantium.

Ivan III and his reign, stretching from 1462-1505, were integral for the creation of the Russian state, earning him the title of "the Great" for tightening the ties between Russia and Byzantium and for propelling Muscovy into dominance by unifying the Russian cities into a true monarchic state. And the conception of Muscovy as an inheritor of Byzantine identity became an idea that has persisted ever since. The double-headed eagle and the title of "tsar" remained features of Russian royalty until its abolition in 1917. Even today, 500 years later, the Byzantine connection rears its double-heads. Tsar Ivan's immediate concerns when his pope-brokered marriage came to fruition have had long-lasting effects that he could not have anticipated.

IVAN'S GRANDSON, ALSO named Ivan, matched him in ambition and energy. Yet he outdid him in the lengths he was willing to go to hold onto this power, solidifying a forceful autocracy that was manifested in his person. What Ivan III had begun, Ivan IV strengthened, finished, and even perfected.[25]

Ivan IV took the throne in 1547 at just 16. Ivan III had used the title "tsar," but for him it was symbolic and tenuous, a nod to his wife's family. But by beginning his reign with a proclamation of divine emperorship, Tsar Ivan IV signaled his absolutism. He was from the outset the sole autocratic ruler of the land, ordained by God to shepherd his people. Orthodox church authorities supported the use of the new title and crowned him with Russian and Byzantine relics to underscore his equivalence to the glorious Roman caesars. In doing so, Ivan IV established the Tsardom of Russia.

Ivan's dictatorship first and foremost served to centralize the Russian state and strengthen his power base. Under his leadership, in 1553, the first Russian printing press began operating. It mainly produced religious propaganda tracts to legitimize his rule. He also curtailed local boyar power, consolidating the collection of cities his grandfather had unified, and established a modern standing army, the *streltsy*, for the defense of Muscovy.

Yet Ivan IV's initiatives were not limited to accumulating internal power. He also expanded Russia's borders, most notably through the conquest of Kazan in 1552. A Mongol/Tatar remnant southeast of Moscow, Kazan was a small, majority-Muslim khanate, centered around the city of the same name. After a month-long siege punctuated by barrages with cutting-edge artillery, Ivan and his army took the city. With one more Tatar vestige destroyed, Russia gained a new metropolitan center on the Volga River, opening up the trading route across the Caspian to Persia, India, and China. Even today, Kazan is a blend of Russian and Central Asian cultures. Rather than a cathedral, Kazan's kremlin is unique in Russia in that it houses a mosque. Many residents have Tatar ancestry and still speak that language.

Given that this was both a religious victory and a continuation of the reconquests of Dmitri Donskoy and Alexander Nevsky, Ivan saw fit to commemorate it in flamboyant style by ordering the construction of a great church in Moscow. St. Basil's Cathedral, the iconic and unmistakable gumdrop-colored, onion-domed building on Red Square, took six years to build and was completed in 1561. According to legend, so proud was Ivan of this construction that he ordered the workers and architects blinded so that they could never produce something so beautiful again.

Ivan IV did not stop there. Sparsely-populated areas on Muscovy's eastern frontier became more settled and were brought into the Russian (and Orthodox) fold. Expeditions began to map out territory east of the Urals, claiming it for Moscow and encouraging settlement. In the west, the Livonian War stabilized Russia's border with the Polish-Lithuanian Commonwealth

---

25. Much of this section draws from Halperin, *Ivan the Terrible*, a relatively new, key source for everything Ivan IV.

and the Baltic states, adding to the Orthodox world areas that were traditionally Catholic. Now Muscovy was not only unified; it was growing in power.

During Ivan's reign, the Tsardom first came into sustained contact with the West. In 1555, an English trading expedition of the Muscovy Company arrived on the shores of the White Sea. After locals discovered the traders and escorted them to the tsar, the merchants met with Ivan, who granted them a monopoly on the export of furs, salt, and other goods. To facilitate this trade, Ivan founded a trading port at Arkhangelsk, on the White Sea. There was just one issue: Arkhangelsk is less than 200 miles from the Arctic Circle and accessible to shipping only by navigating north of Scandinavia. For nearly half of the year, the route is packed with ice, which forced merchants to revert to river- and land-based trade. Regardless, ties with foreign powers demonstrated that Ivan IV saw himself and his country as ready to engage with the rest of Europe by either the coin or sword.

While Ivan ushered in stability and prestige for himself and the Russian state, it came at a cost. Unquestioned, unilateral authority had to be upheld, which meant that dissent could not be tolerated.

The clearest touchstone of Ivan's autocratic tendencies was his creation of the *oprichnina*. The name has no clear meaning in Russian, but the *oprichnina* could be considered one of the world's earliest secret police forces. Dressed in monastic-style black robes and hand-picked by Ivan from among the boyar class, members of the force were tasked with punishing those who ran afoul of the tsar. Their insignia were dogs' heads and brooms, symbolic of watching over the realm and sweeping out insubordination. A Russian, especially a boyar, who spoke ill of the tsar or did something to enrich himself at the tsar's expense could find himself imprisoned, forcibly sent to a monastery to live out the rest of his life in pious obscurity, tortured, or killed.

Adding to the image of a paranoid, power-hungry tyrant who demanded complete loyalty is a bizarre exercise: Ivan liked to test the loyalty of his entourage by pretending to abdicate, and then returning to the throne at the "behest" of the people. Records show that he did this at least twice, but it is possible that it occurred more often. The false abdications were perhaps designed so that nobles felt safe to put their true feelings on the table, flushing out anyone who might question the tsar. But questions linger about this habit. Could this be evidence that Ivan was an unstable and abusive ruler?

More evidence for Ivan's iron fist can be found in how he finally brought Novgorod to heel. Even after Ivan III's conquest, the city chafed under Moscow's rule. In 1569, Novgorodian dissent boiled over into open rebellion, spurred by plague, famine, war, and *oprichnina* repression. Ivan IV responded by ordering a military sack of the city and a massacre of its population. He then split the city between direct control by his government and rule by *oprichnina* officials, as if it were a conquered and occupied foreign stronghold. Deaths are estimated to have numbered in the tens of thousands. Public buildings were looted, and

Two views of a complicated figure: calculating leader (Viktor Vasnetsov, 1897, left) and crazed despot (detail, Ilya Repin, 1885).

Novgorod was forever after integrated into the larger Russian state. Any potential for future republican independence was put down by the sword.[26]

Shortly after the sack of Novgorod, the *oprichnina* were disbanded. Apparently, the inhumane behavior of *oprichnina* members was so extreme that Ivan was forced to admit that the institution had no place in his court.

It was not for nothing that Ivan IV earned the epithet "the Terrible." He is often held up as the paragon of Russian autocracy, the dictatorial, overbearing, oppressive leader, precursor to later Stalins and Putins. This is not helped by the fact that the Russian word translated as

---

26. Curiously, Ivan IV summoned a *zemsky sobor*, or "council of the land," several times during his reign, which called together boyars from throughout Russia to debate and approve his initiatives. This was the earliest representative political body in Russia.

"terrible," grozny, is more accurately understood as "dreaded," "foreboding," or "terrifying." Ivan IV has a legacy that is almost universally negative.[27]

The reality is, however, that Ivan's life and legacy are much more complex than simply "good" or "bad," or even "terrible." Two portraits painted nearly 300 years after his death represent the two personalities Ivan IV has come to embody. One is Viktor Vasnetsov's portrait, with a scowling tsar descending a staircase in full regalia, glaring at the viewer under a heavy, brutish brow. The other, Ilya Repin's interpretation of the (possibly apocryphal) story of Ivan fatally striking his heir, has a dark background, as Ivan clutches his son, his crazed eyes and frantic hair all that is visible of his face. Just like he is portrayed in these 19th-century paintings, we still see him today as a ruler who was calculated, stolid, and severe, and at the same time fickle, superstitious, and even, possibly, insane. Yet scholars today continue to debate his life and legacy. The real Ivan has been dwarfed by myths and legends that have formed an impenetrable cocoon of mystique around him. But was he truly and "worse" than other monarchs of the time, like Henry VIII, Charles V, and Francis I? It is nearly impossible to grasp the real, unadulterated person of Ivan IV.

And, in spite of Ivan IV's popular image as a bloodthirsty tyrant, in recent years some have tried to rehabilitate the image of Ivan, playing up his contributions as a founding figure in Russian history. To this end, statues to Ivan have appeared, immortalizing the "terrible" ruler. The first was christened in 2016 in the town of Oryol, a town Ivan founded not far from Moscow. A riverside city park in front of a historic church was chosen as the home of an equestrian figure of the tsar. Following a ceremony to officially christen the statue in 2020, Russia's Minister of Culture explained that the statue commemorates Ivan the Terrible as "one of the most controversial yet outstanding figures in Russia's history. During the years of his leadership, he managed to take a number of bold and decisive steps aimed at the strengthening of unity of the Russian state."[28]

Vandals were quick to strike, pointing out Ivan's atrocities by spattering fake blood on the statue and hanging a deprecating sign around its neck. In the Siberian city of Kansk, an activist erected a blood-soaked wooden stake on the local river as a counterpart to Oryol's homage, tipping the hat to Ivan's proclivity for cruelty in a way that some deemed more apt. Another Ivan statue, a simple and unpretentious bust, was installed with little fanfare in Moscow in 2017.

IF IVAN IV was the prototypical tyrant, his rule made legitimate through blood and embodying the centralized Russian power first realized under Ivan III, then the next chapter of Russia's story highlighted the necessity of that autocracy. Within just a few years, the impenetrable Tsardom shattered into centerless disorder.

---

27. One need look no further than *Night at the Museum 2*.

28. Borodin, "Pamiatnik Ivanu Groznomu otkryl v Orle."

Ivan's personal life did not create a suitable environment to pass along his realm seamlessly. Ivan had three sons from three different wives (of seven wives total): from oldest to youngest, Ivan, Feodor, and Dmitri. His eldest was set to take the throne, but died young, if the legend is to be believed, by his enraged father's hand. This is the scene Repin portrays in his painting: Ivan's eyes betraying remorse at what cannot be undone. More likely, the heir simply died from disease.

When Ivan IV died of a stroke in 1584 at age 53, 27-year-old Feodor became tsar. However, it was soon apparent that he would not wield power as his father had. Feodor was a gentle and pious man who made an irresolute and weak ruler. Scholars speculate that he may have been afflicted by an intellectual disability. Nonetheless, he took the reins of the Russian Tsardom.

The third son, Dmitri, was three when his father died and was living with his mother in the town of Uglich, far from Moscow. Advisors close to Feodor assured him that they had orchestrated Dmitri's death, lest the tsar's rule be insecure.

Back in the capital, Tsar Feodor was in good hands. Before his death, Ivan IV had asked a trio of advisors to guide Feodor in his rule, and the young tsar was happy to let someone else do the governing for him. Among these advisors was Boris Godunov, Feodor's brother-in-law. Godunov had been an insider in Ivan IV's court but had gained enough influence with Feodor to become a trusted confidant, often acting on the new tsar's behalf with few restrictions. The other two advisors were elbowed away from the throne. While Feodor acted the part of tsar, Godunov became the true power behind the scenes.

When Feodor died in 1598 with no heir and no remaining brothers or half-brothers, Godunov saw an opportunity. He was already the acting ruler, so, when a council of powerful boyars convened to select the new tsar, he was a shoo-in. In 1598 Godunov was crowned the first non-Rurikid ruler of Russia.

Yet not all Muscovite nobles supported Godunov. Led by the old-money Romanov boyar clan, a minority coalition saw Godunov as an opportunistic usurper rather than a rightful heir to the Tsardom. But they were sharply outnumbered both by other boyars and the commoners. The Romanovs and their allies were forced to flee Moscow.

Godunov was an adept statesman, and his governing skill became apparent quickly. Yet he soon faced insurmountable challenges. A world away, in Peru, a volcanic eruption led to a period of global cooling. In Russia, the summer of 1601 simply never arrived. Harvests failed. Famine hit Russia and stretched on for two years. It is estimated that starvation led to the deaths of two million Russians, a third of the total population.

Many desperate commoners fled to Moscow in hopes of a better lot. This resulted in overcrowding, disease, and economic upheaval in the city, feeding dissatisfaction towards Godunov and his rule. Some peasants joined groups of brigands, like the Cossacks, bands of escaped and free serfs who lived a nomadic lifestyle in the open steppes of southern Russia along the Don and Volga Rivers. In turn, the Cossacks, desperate, raided towns and cities, stealing whatever they needed. With Moscow already strained, a military response was

False Dmitri I defenestrates himself in an 1879 painting by Carl Wenig.

infeasible, and so lawlessness added to the civil unrest. Godunov's legitimacy, which, as a non-Rurikid, had never been completely solid, was evaporating.

This created the opportunity for an outsider to play on Russians' dissatisfaction. In 1600, a young man appeared in Moscow claiming to be the now-teenage Dmitri of Uglich, the late Tsar Feodor's half-brother. He claimed to have miraculously escaped murder at the hands of Godunov's lackeys, gone into hiding, and now returned as the true heir to the throne as a son of Ivan IV. "Dmitri" traveled the countryside garnering support almost as soon as the famine began. Many commoners threw their support behind him as a viable and preferable alternative to Godunov.

When Godunov ordered the troublemaker arrested for interrogation, "Dmitri" fled to the Polish-Lithuanian Commonwealth. When he arrived, the Polish court welcomed him in.

Polish nobility sensed a chance to bring the weakened Russia under their control and officially endorsed his claim to the throne, denouncing Godunov as a usurper himself.

In a poor coincidence of timing, in 1604, only a year after Poland endorsed Dmitri's claim, Godunov died. His son abdicated, not wanting to shoulder the burden of the Tsardom in its current state. In response, "Dmitri," along with thousands of Polish troops, frustrated Russian boyars, starving Russian citizens, and Cossacks, triumphantly entered the Moscow Kremlin with no resistance. "Dmitri" was crowned and in July 1605 sat himself on the Russian throne.

Tsar Dmitri I was, from the get-go, a Polish puppet, a close associate of Russia's archenemies: the Catholic Poles. Once his policies began to explicitly reflect a pro-Polish and anti-Orthodox bias, his subjects became angry. Notably, Dmitri's new Catholic wife was not forced to become Orthodox after marriage, as had been tradition since Vladimir I. A mob of boyars and Muscovites stormed the Kremlin, baying for blood. Breaching the walls, they made directly for the palace. In a panicked attempt to escape, Dmitri jumped out a high window, breaking his leg on the street below. Crippled, he was overrun by the frenzied rabble and torn to pieces. The remains were then shot from a cannon pointed westward, toward Poland.

Thus, in May 1606, the rule of the first "false Dmitri" came to an end. If his claim was correct and he really was Ivan IV's son, he died at the age of 23. But his death left a power vacuum. Poland maintained its hold on the Russian lands, so a new tsar was placed on the throne who would support Polish aims: Vasily Shuisky. To prevent Vasily from meeting the same end as Dmitri, Polish troops were sent to occupy Russia, ensuring that the cities recognized the new tsar.

Two years later, a second Dmitri made a grab for the throne. Despite grumbling under Shuisky, Russians rejected this Dmitri and so he saw little success. Polish forces rooted him out and put him to death. In 1612, a third Dmitri arose, once again promising the overthrow of the Polish elite. His support fizzled despite help from some of the Cossack bands. He, too, was found and killed by the Polish overlords. The efforts of a fourth Dmitri who appeared later that year dissolved quickly, likely due in no small part to waning gullibility on the part of the everyday Russian. He was the final claimant to the house of Ivan IV.

By 1611, after years of occupation, the Russians had had enough. With the famine over and the Poles unwelcome occupiers, it was time to take up the sword. A resistance army gathered in the town of Nizhny Novgorod, far to the east of the seat of Polish power in Moscow.[29] It was led by a Muscovite noble, Dmitri Pozharsky, and funded by a local merchant, Kuzma Minin. Together, they mustered a ragtag army of Russian rebels, dispossessed nobles, and angry Cossacks.

Pozharsky led the troops on an extended military campaign, beating back Polish forces as they went. When they finally reached Moscow, they found the citizens already rebelling

---

29. Not to be confused with the other Novgorod. "Nizhny Novgorod" is a river trade port on the Volga east of Moscow. Its name means "Lower Novgorod" or "Lesser Novgorod." The ancient "Veliky" or "Great Novgorod," Rurik's home on the Volkhov, is to the northwest, near modern St. Petersburg.

Minin and Pozharsky in brass conversation, Moscow, with Ivan IV's St. Basil's Cathedral in the background. Photo credit: Alexander Tolstykh (Dreamstime).

against the Polish officials. The mob, hearing of Pozharsky's success, had forced the Poles to hole up in the Kremlin. Pozharsky and his army joined the siege.

It took 19 months to starve out the occupiers; reportedly, some resorted to cannibalism. Finally, on November 6, 1612, the Polish garrison surrendered, leaving the city in disgrace. Moscow was Russia's once more. Minin and Pozharsky earned an immortal spot as Russian folk heroes for saving Russia and expelling the invaders. A statue of the pair stands on Red Square before Ivan IV's St. Basil's Cathedral, eternally admonishing each other to defend their homeland.

With Moscow recaptured and the Poles at bay, the boyars set about discussing who to install as the new tsar. After deliberation, they settled on young Mikhail Romanov, a member of the ancient trading family that had fled when Godunov was installed as tsar. Mikhail was called to the capital by the boyar council and crowned in the Kremlin on his 17th birthday, July 22, 1613, ending the Time of Troubles. The ceremony was overseen by the highest levels of Orthodox officialdom.

With the reinstitution of centralized power, the new tsars forged a Russia even stronger than before. For much of the 17th century, under Mikhail and his Romanov successors, Alexis (reigned 1645-76) and Feodor III (reigned 1676-82), Russia consolidated its power, brushing aside its enemies, putting down rebellions, and rebuilding the potent state apparatus that had been lost in the turmoil. By 1650, Russia's borders reached the Pacific, making it one of the largest nations of the time, stretching from Kiev, the Caucasus Mountains, and the Volga Steppe to the border of China.

THE ROMANOV DYNASTY lasted until 1917, a total of 304 years. Yet, according to legend, Mikhail's reign was in danger of destruction before it could even get off the ground. It was saved only through the selfless patriotism of a poor forester.

It is said that the Polish royal family, on hearing of Mikhail Romanov's nomination as tsar, were infuriated at the prospect of losing Russia for good. They vowed reprisal, sending a small army into Russia in February 1613 to retake Moscow for Poland. Mikhail Romanov had not yet left the monastery in Kostroma to which his family had been exiled, and it was there the Poles sought to accost him, before he could receive the crown and inspire the unity of the people. Time was of the essence, so the Polish force had to move quickly.

On a frigid late-night march after hours on the road, the Poles stumbled across an elderly logger by the name of Ivan Susanin. He offered to show the commanders a shortcut to the monastery where Mikhail was living, and the Poles, cold and exhausted and lost, agreed to the offer. Susanin set out at the head of the army. Neither he nor the Polish force were ever heard from again. His countrymen theorized, and later accepted as fact, that he had led the Polish troops deep into the forest and away from the new tsar, where they discovered his ruse and killed him before becoming lost in the wild, never to emerge.

Whether or not Ivan Susanin actually existed, his action demonstrated a high degree of devotion to Russia's new ruler. Susanin was willing to sacrifice himself not so much for who Mikhail Romanov was – after all, he had yet to take the throne when Susanin guided the Polish troops into the woods – but more for the idea of a centrally-controlled Russian state, one that was stable, powerful, and prosperous. One that was the antithesis of Russia in the Time of Troubles.

Susanin and the values he manifested were immortalized in an 1836 opera by Mikhail Glinka called *A Life for the Tsar*. The theme of the story – personal sacrifice for the sake of a God-chosen absolute monarch – only made the opera more popular among Russia's upper classes of the Imperial period. Susanin became an example to be emulated.

If Ivan III and Ivan IV represent imperial splendor through concentrated power, the rudderless years of the Time of Troubles embody their opposite. When the boyars righted the ship, they must have acknowledged that the chaos, death, and lawlessness of the Smuta, as it is called in Russia, was in no small part caused by weak leadership. In the absence of a sacred autocrat, Russia had almost ceased to exist. The themes of this period – power and lawlessness, order and anarchy, sacred duty and neglect – haunted Russia for centuries after. The lesson emerged clear as day: centralized power is critical to the continued existence of the Russian state.

Yet while the Russia of the early Romanovs had recovered, it was merely a regional power. The centralization of Ivan IV had become stale, and Russia, once more isolated in the wake of the Time of Troubles, was far from a modern international powerhouse. It would take an unlikely, gangly, raucous, and forward-thinking Romanov to change that.

HOW RUSSIA GREW

5

MODERNIZATION: RUSSIA IN THE IMAGE OF PETER AND CATHERINE

Russia before Peter | Peter and his half-siblings | Looking to the West | Catherine, the other Great | The tragicomedy of Paul I

The Russia that Peter I inherited was very similar to that created by Ivan IV. The Tsardom was an autocratic, centralized state, with close ties between the church and the divine-right tsar. But while this was common among European powers in the 16th century, by the late 17th, Russia was an exception.

For most of Europe, this was the age of exploration, colonialism, religious reformation, Enlightenment, and even stirrings of industry. Russia had left behind its Time of Troubles, but had barely moved further forward. With no university, a culture and religion that discouraged science, a single, subarctic trade port, an army that was a vestige of Ivan IV's time, and no ships except a few riverboats commandeered in times of need, it was, by some measures, backward.

Peter I worked tirelessly to make Russia modern, to imbue it with enough pride that it could stand shoulder-to-shoulder with the greatest European empires of the day. By his own force of will, he dragged Russia, kicking and screaming, into the 18th century. And what Peter began, his granddaughter Catherine would later bring to fruition. Yet these two rulers, both later styled "the Great," only brought into sharper focus persistent questions of nationality, modernity, autocracy, and freedom.

While Peter's reforms were overdue, they were not inevitable. His path to the throne, and thence to greatness, was a complicated one.[30]

THE THIRD ROMANOV tsar, Feodor III, died without an heir in 1682. Seeking to avoid a repeat of the Time of Troubles, the nobility looked to the descendants of his predecessor and father, Alexis, for new rulers. They had options. Alexis I had left behind two clans from two wives: the Naryshkins and Miloslavskys. Each boasted an eligible young male heir with a legitimate claim to the throne: Peter Naryshkin and Ivan Miloslavsky.

---

30. For an overview on Peter, see Massie, *Peter the Great*.

But Alexis I's cunning daughter from the Miloslavsky line, Sophia, inserted herself in front of both heirs. After gaining the support of the *streltsy*, Ivan IV's professional military corps, she made her bid for royal power.

With two legitimate male heirs, however, Sophia's rule was out of the question. Sophia had to back away from taking full control, calculating that it would be better to retain some power through compromise than lose it all by being stubborn. But there was a loophole. By endorsing her brother Ivan's right to the throne, Sophia could act as regent over the 16-year-old and immature Ivan V. While not quite as prestigious as full *tsaritsa*, it was better than nothing.

There was, however, one more catch. Ivan was young, but already he promised to be infirm, soft, and simple. To ensure proper rulership, and appease the boyars and Naryshkins, Sophia's and Ivan's half-brother Peter, age 10, was to rule as co-tsar, alongside Ivan, until such time as both grew up and the situation could be decided for good.

Sophia acquiesced begrudgingly. She ordered a throne engineered that was large enough to seat both of the young co-tsars on a bench, with a compartment in the back for Sophia to sit in to advise the two of them, whispering in their ears. While Ivan and Peter were the faces, Sophia was the brains.[31]

Understandably, the Naryshkins felt stung by Sophia, who had so brutishly and unscrupulously inserted herself onto, or rather behind, the Russian throne. But the young co-tsar Peter did not seem to mind. He preferred spending his time in other ways rather than sitting in court. Peter was an active and intensely intelligent boy who loved sailing on Russia's lakes and rivers. He showed a keen interest in Western shipbuilding and military standardization. Some stories even say he organized his friends, the children of other noble families, into strictly-regulated armies and pitted themselves against each other, using leather balls fired from cannons instead of the real thing.

Peter soon grew into a young man, standing nearly seven feet tall. Official contemporary portraits show him as slender, which he undoubtedly was. More accurate and less flattering representations show him with a small head, a wispy mustache, long legs, and gangly arms, and he leaned forward when he walked, which made him appear longer. He was hardworking, enthusiastic, and focused, a natural leader among his peers despite his strange appearance.

As he got older, the boyars began to see that Peter would make an excellent tsar, and that Ivan and Sophia would have to step aside. Sophia, naturally, rejected the idea, and began plotting to secure her place through violence. In 1689, Peter and his Naryshkin family fled Moscow to escape the danger. In his absence, allies in the capital overthrew Sophia and sent her to a nunnery to live out the rest of her life as a permanent guest. The half-brothers Ivan and Peter thus became true co-tsars with no regent behind the scenes. Soon, though, Ivan's poor physical and mental health caught up with him. He died in 1696, when Peter was 24.

---

31. This throne can still be seen today in the Kremlin Armory in Moscow.

And so Peter became the sole ruler of the Tsardom of Russia.

The new tsar began his reign by leaving his homeland altogether, embarking on a "Grand Embassy" only a year after rising to the throne. Peter and his entourage set out to explore Europe in a massive months-long tour. In Holland, a major trading republic, Peter disguised himself as a common laborer to work in the shipyard, studying closely the latest techniques for building strong and swift vessels for the world's globe-trotting navies. In Prussia, a military powerhouse, he met with some of the finest strategists and battlefield commanders in the world. In England, he visited national institutions of higher education and science, like the Royal Observatory at Greenwich.[32]

Emboldened by Peter's absence, Sophia organized her forces from inside her nunnery cell. She coordinated with loyal *streltsy* regiments to free her and take the Kremlin, but Peter's forces intercepted and defeated them in a pitched battle. As punishment, Sophia formally became a nun rather than a mere prisoner. Peter, relaying orders from the road, had her treasonous court allies strung up just outside her cell window so that she could see their decaying bodies swaying in the wind each time she looked outside. In retribution for their insubordination, the *streltsy*, the last holdout of the old Russian army established by Ivan the Terrible, faced torture, death, and disbandment. Sophia died in the nunnery in 1704.

Peter returned to Russia energized and determined to remake Russia as a European power. The young tsar started with an ambitious new plan: the construction of a European-style capital. Moscow was dour, insular, and medieval, stinking of Orthodox incense, cloaked in the backward mysticism of fur-lined kaftans and the ominous scepter of ancient princes, with an imposing fortress and winding streets lined with dark stone houses. It was also far from the sea, the open gate to the outside world. Cities like London and Amsterdam, on the other hand, were massive ports with fresh architecture that followed the latest research in urban planning, bustling trade centers with famed universities and museums and government offices. He had seen them firsthand. Peter's new city, he resolved, would be a thoroughly modern endeavor.

Peter hand-picked its location: a set of low-lying islands at the mouth of the Neva River, at the eastern end of the Baltic Sea, near where Alexander Nevsky had fought the legendary battle that had earned him his nickname. A large, protected bay led to the open ocean, granting easy access to Europe and thence to the world. It was not only more hospitable to shipping than Arkhangelsk; the Neva could serve as a natural highway inland as it snaked from the sea into the very core of the Russian land.

There was just one problem: this territory and its surrounds were under Swedish control, then one of the region's foremost powers. To establish a Russian town, much less a capital, on

---

32. He also, reportedly, totally trashed the English country house where he and his friends were staying. They destroyed the flooring, trampled the garden, and irreparably damaged priceless artwork. Peter was quite a party animal. Depending on the account, his "All-Joking, All-Drunken Synod of Fools and Jesters" was either a massive but innocent fraternity of eager drinking buddies or a secret, sinister society fueled by satirical dwarves, flowing alcohol, and unconventional sex. See Farquhar, *Secret Lives of the Tsars*, 38.

the site would require this land to fall into Russian hands. And so war was declared in 1700, with the capture of this Baltic territory as one of Peter's main goals.

Peter leaned on his European experiences, and the new Russian army, freshly raised to European standards of tactics, drill, and dress, was more than a match for the Swedes. In May 1703 a small Swedish fort at the mouth of the river was captured easily by Russian forces, and Peter immediately ordered the construction of a much larger stone bastion. It marked the heart of the city Peter planned: St. Petersburg.[33]

With Sweden out of the Neva's delta, Peter had a blank canvas on which to construct his vision. But building the city was far from simple. When the area was not outright frozen, it was soggy and impassable. In summer, it was a breeding ground for mosquitoes and the diseases they bore, and in winter, it was penetratingly frigid, dark, and wet. Still, Peter persisted in this unlikely and unfriendly location, ordering the importation of workers and materials to fuel the project. It is estimated that as many as 25,000 peasants and artisans died through forced labor, freezing, and sickness to build St. Petersburg.

From its very beginning, St. Petersburg was designed to be a state-of-the-art city of its time, and Peter used the unlimited power at his disposal as tsar to accomplish this. Stone, absent in the area, was key to creating stable foundations in the shifting estuary, so Peter forbade any stone construction outside the new capital, often expropriating these resources by force. Any visitor to the city was forced to pay a "stone tax": arriving ships were required to bring a set number of blocks with them for use in the quixotic metropolis. The city's long, straight avenues crossed at planned angles, breaking up grids into neighborhoods and creating regular city blocks, shopping centers, and parks. Two main arteries ended at the gleaming spire of the Admiralty Building, a monumental symbol of another Petrine brainchild: a Russian navy. Sailing ships and naval forts, while no match for the British and French, were all administered from the Admiralty and the nearby island christened Kronstadt, like St. Petersburg a faux-Germanic name concocted by Peter. At the core of the city was Peter and Paul Fortress, with squat defensive walls per the latest military theory, guarding the Neva and the water passages into the Russian interior.

Peter imported the finest Italian architects to help construct his new capital. They brought with them the latest in neoclassical design for civic spaces, building a city more Roman than Russian. To encourage drainage and ease construction, canals criss-crossed the city, adding a romantic, Venetian flair.[34] The city center soon boasted all the magnificent urban palaces, museums, military and scientific academies, theaters, printing presses, government bureaus,

---

33. Peter's choice of name was odd. In Russian, pronounced "*Sankt-Piterboorg*," it has no meaning. It is a vaguely German-Dutch-sounding name that happens to incorporate the name of its founder and sound a little like it means "St. Peter's City." Today, many Russians call it "Petersburg," or, if they are especially fond of it, just "Peter," as if it is an old friend. See Miles, *St. Petersburg*, for a deep dive into the history of the city and its impact on the course of Russian history.

34. These did little to prevent catastrophic floods that inundated the city with dirty and freezing water well into the 20th century.

riverside promenades, and manicured parks Peter had seen in Europe on his Grand Embassy. Bustling wharves bristled with masts of ships from far corners of the earth. The port of St. Petersburg, Russia's window to the West, was open for business.

In 1712, Peter officially moved his court from Moscow to St. Petersburg. Nobles were bribed and, in some cases, simply forced from their comfortable Moscow digs to what was at the time not much more than a muddy construction site. Yet St. Petersburg slowly took shape as the Amsterdam clone Peter had envisioned. Moscow retained its role as the spiritual heart of Russia, the go-to spot for coronations and headquarters for the Orthodox Church, but the political arm of the Russian court had moved. It was further added to and embellished by the generations of rulers who followed Peter I.

A quintessential portrait of Peter I, highlighting his ambitious countenance, drawn from life in 1717 by Carl de Moor.

ALONG WITH HIS European-style capital, Peter imposed several laws to create a European-style nation. Gone was the traditional garb of the gentry. Rather than wearing long sleeves that covered the hands, denoting someone who did not work, nobles adopted the more functional European dress of the time: coats, wigs, and breeches. In an effort to rid his nation of old-fashioned facial hair in favor of more fashionable mustaches or clean-shaven faces, Peter taxed upper-class beards by their length. Wealthy women, once relegated to a cloistered upstairs suite called a *terem*, were now permitted greater freedom to associate, learn, and participate in public activities. Rather than raucous medieval feasts, nobles held refined balls with Viennese waltzes, sporting the latest fashions from Paris. In addition, Peter created the Holy Synod, a group of bishops to oversee the Russian Orthodox Church. The synod was answerable to the tsar alone, effectively making him the supreme leader of the church. The move brought the relationship between church and state closer while also paving the way for the Church to function as an appendage of the crown.

The early 18th century also marked a cultural shift from religious to more diversified and secular subjects in Russia. Western-style opera and theater were established and embraced by the upper classes, and Russian painting turned from flat icon-like portraits with almost exclusively religious subjects to classically-inspired Italian-style realism with a dose of Dutch maritime painting and landscapes. Peter's new St. Petersburg University, the first in Russia, and his Kunstkammer Museum began to attract scientific attention and train the populace in the latest enlightenment thought. Now, those running the state could embrace the learning of the West. Administrators, engineers, and thinkers were cultivated through education, creating a new professional class.

Yet, for all his modernizing, Peter did not touch one of the most deeply entrenched institutions in Russia. Serfdom was the economic foundation of the country and had remained essentially unchanged for hundreds of years. Many of those who had died building St. Petersburg had been little more than slaves, either owned by the state or tied for life to wealthy nobles. Further, Peter's governing style fully embodied the Russian tradition of sacred absolutist monarchy, making almost no overtures towards the limited sovereignty of Great Britain or the Netherlands. As tsar, Peter wielded limitless power, just as Ivan IV had done. But one does not take a swamp and make it a city while paying attention to checks and balances.

The war with Sweden finally ended in 1721 with the Battle of Poltava, where Peter's modernized army decisively quashed a Swedish incursion. With victory in hand, Peter declared himself Emperor of Russia, in the Western style. After all, Russia had proved that it was now a great power. And St. Petersburg, the city that had not existed two decades before, was the capital of the modernized Russian Empire.

Over Peter's lifetime, Russia changed dramatically. Peter's tireless reforms, inexhaustible energy, and overarching drive to see Russia modernized made the Tsardom about-face near-instantaneously, historically speaking. He is one of the single most influential characters in Russia's story, a keystone, and he is remembered as such.

THERE IS A debate among foreigners who travel to Russia over which city is better: Moscow or St. Petersburg. Many love Moscow, and it is easy to see why. Moscow is home to Russia's government, a bustling world-class city that is constantly evolving and changing. It has an energy that is fast-paced, dynamic, and optimistic.

But St. Petersburg wins out for many (this author included). Its bizarre origin, born from a visionary who defied all logic, created an impractical metropolis that is self-consciously a construction of itself, still bearing imago Peter 300 years later. Its vibe is slower, more introspective, a little shabbier. While Moscow, clad in a suit and Rolex, frantically types between sips of a Starbucks latte, sweater-clad Petersburg curls up in a well-worn armchair with tea and a good book as it drizzles outside. It need not impress. Everyone sees it for what it is: an 18th-century Disneyland copy of European metropolises, one that is perhaps past its glory days. But it revels in it, it owns it. For this reason, St. Petersburg has emerged as the backdrop of several classic works of Russian literature. Where better to put a fairy tale, gritty, desperate, or surreal, than in a magical, impossible, dream-born castle?

Peter had found St. Petersburg a landscape of mud and left it a city of stone. But Peter's family matters stand in contrast to the lush grounds of his homes and the orderly symmetry

Two of Peter's contributions today, along the Neva River: the domed tower of the Kunstkammer (left) and the tall spire of the Peter and Paul Fortress (right) on a quintessential St. Petersburg summer night. Photo credit: Yulia Baturina (Dreamstime).

of his city's streets. Peter's eldest son and heir apparent, Alexei, had a poor relationship with his father. When Alexei plotted with foreign powers to revert Russia back to its conservative roots, he was imprisoned and tortured. Death was the appropriate sentence, but his execution could only be confirmed by his father's signature. Peter hesitated, seemingly unable to let his son die by his hand. So Alexei passed away slowly in captivity.

Thus, before Peter himself died in 1724, at 52 and with no male heir, he gave the empire to his second wife, who reigned as Catherine I. She and her successors – Peter II, Anna, and Elizabeth – built on the work Peter had started, while retaining absolute power, for good or ill. For much of the 18th century, these tsars and *tsaritsa*s founded universities, worked alongside some of the greatest scientists of their day, allied themselves with European powers, continued building St. Petersburg, and patronized the arts. Russian life continued to move Westward, prodded along by supportive rulers.

At the same time, though, the post-Petrine tsars could be eccentric and cruel. Legend has it that Empress Anna loved hunting so much that she kept loaded muskets on the Hermitage windowsills to take potshots at pigeons. Another tale relates that she once married a disgraced nobleman to one of her uglier maids and forced the two of them to spend their wedding night in a building made completely of ice on the frozen Neva River. The couple survived the ordeal, just barely. Anna faced no consequences.

When Anna died, the imperial crown went briefly to her two-month-old nephew, Ivan VI, before one of Peter's daughters, Elizabeth, effected a coup; according to one telling, she herself led the storming of the palace wearing an antique breastplate and brandishing a crucifix. Elizabeth's time as empress set the stage for the Russian autocrat of the era that truly embodied Peter the Great's values: Catherine II, also known as Catherine the Great. But her story began far from Russia.

EMPRESS ELIZABETH CHOSE her heir from a young age. The future Peter III was her nephew and a grandson of Peter I. He seemed the perfect candidate, with an excellent pedigree, to be declared emperor upon Elizabeth's death. In 1742, the teenage Peter took up residence in the sprawling, idyllic Oranienbaum Palace outside St. Petersburg. There, he had access to a fine court education to prepare him for his role as Russia's next emperor.

A bride was soon found for Peter: 16-year-old Sophia Augusta Frederica, the bookish and intelligent daughter of a minor but ambitious German lord. She spoke not a word of Russian, but nonetheless she arrived for her marriage in 1745. When, per tradition, she converted to Orthodoxy, she took on the name Catherine. As she settled into her new life among Russian royalty, she closely studied her new homeland, likely to avoid her husband, whom she quickly came to loathe.

Even as a teenager, Peter III was mean and cruel, taking childish pleasure in ordering around his household. He had Empress Anna's biting sense of humor and a proclivity for drink, qualities that were not softened by his smallpox-scarred face and the bitterness he

The Hermitage, St. Petersburg, in more recent years. Beginning in the mid-18th century, the palace was the Romanovs' chief urban residence. The squat, yellow building on the left is Peter's Admiralty. Photo credit: Sgorin2009 (Dreamstime).

harbored because of it. Rather than valuing Russia while integrating facets of the West to strengthen it, Peter wholly disdained his home country and was instead enamored with German military pomp. He took little interest in government, playing with toy soldiers well into adulthood rather than leading real soldiers. An older Catherine recalled how she once entered his chambers to find a rat swinging from a tiny gallows. Peter explained that the rat had bitten off the head of one of his miniature soldiers and so had been hanged for treason.

Catherine found rooms for herself on the opposite side of the palace. Both Peter and Catherine took extramarital lovers. There is even debate as to whether they ever consummated their marriage. If the rumors are true, then the Romanov line ended here.

Almost immediately after Elizabeth's death in 1762, the true character of Peter was put on full display. Russia had for five years been embroiled in the Seven Years' War, a massive conflict involving most of the European powers and rending the established diplomatic order. North America, Southeast Asia, and Europe were seeing bloody battles on a massive scale played out by a dizzying kaleidoscope of shifting alliances. It was an opportunity for Peter III, now emperor at age 35, to flex his ruling chops and demonstrate to his subjects that he was tsar material. A conclusive military success would legitimize his rule and garner the unified support of his subjects.

Instead, he promptly switched sides in the conflict, withdrawing Russian troops from occupied lands and allying with his adored Prussia. This move upset the balance of power and handed Prussia a last-minute victory. The war was over, but Peter's credibility was undermined.

Catherine saw an opening. Rallying palace guards to her side, she and officers loyal to her deposed Peter. She was installed in his place as Empress Catherine II. Peter had reigned for only six months.

Catherine II immediately demonstrated that she was, like Peter I, ambitious, energetic, and a strong believer in Enlightenment ideals. Her years at Oranienbaum had given her ample time to read the latest thinking of the day coming out of Western universities, which discussed in depth the roles and duties of the state and citizen. By the time she became empress, she was well equipped to take what Peter the Great had set out to do and bring it to full fruition.

Catherine launched several progressive initiatives, pouring funding and patronage into the arts and sciences. New universities were opened throughout Russia, including the Smolny Institute of Noble Maidens, one of the first public schools for women in Europe. She also founded dozens of new hospitals and promoted inoculation as a means of preventing disease. Before long, some of the world's best professors, musicians, and doctors were walking St. Petersburg's streets, attracted by the opportunities Catherine had opened up. The Russian Empire became a beacon of science, medicine, and art. A further break with the Orthodox past came when Catherine confiscated monastic property in 1763. Of some 2,000 active monasteries in the late 17th century, by 1764, only 318 remained.[35]

Catherine cultivated the image of an enlightened autocrat: a despot with absolute power, yet with the wisdom to wield that power in the best interests of her people. She corresponded with the French philosopher Voltaire and encouraged her court to engage with the latest thinking of the times. Catherine herself published works on philosophy that grappled with some of the big political-science questions of her day. Her renovations to the Catherine Palace, originally built for Peter I's wife, included the construction of a pavilion designed for debate, complete with busts of famous historical thinkers to inspire high-quality rhetoric.

Catherine's reign was not bloodless. In fact, for all her enlightenment, Catherine oversaw some of Russia's most aggressive expansion. A campaign in what is today Ukraine annexed the Crimean Khanate, the final Mongol holdout closely associated with the Ottoman Turks, and the addition of those lands, called "Novorossiya," or New Russia, to the Russian Empire. Crucially, through this conquest, Russia gained a port in the Crimean Peninsula, allowing for maritime access to the Mediterranean. The empire now extended even further southwest, almost into the Balkans, and Russia eyed Constantinople, to which the Third Rome held a dubious claim. While Catherine never pursued that ambition, the dream of a Russian neo-Byzantine Constantinople remained alive in the Russian psyche.

---

35. Billington, *Icon and the Axe*, 201.

The unhappy couple: Catherine and Peter before either had reached the throne in a contemporary painting by Georg Grooth.

When it came to internal policies, Catherine was no more merciful. In 1773, a Cossack by the name of Yemelyan Pugachev led a rebellion and took over a slice of the steppe region, freeing serfs, executing landowners and nobles, and claiming territory as a self-governing state. In response to this threat to her realm, Catherine's armies were quick to restore order at the cold tip of a bayonet. Further, serfdom remained a deep-seated Russian institution.

As with Peter I, Catherine had a conception of herself and her role as empress that centered on autocracy as an untouchable institution. Yet while Peter had sought to emulate German and North European commerce and military science, Catherine found common cause with the absolutist Bourbon monarchs in France and studied the apologists of their glorious rule. When stirrings of revolution began in Paris towards the end of her reign, Catherine was quick to tighten censorship and head off any potential unrest by force. She turned her back on her beloved France and instead embraced Russia's already-long tradition of draconian repression.

One of Catherine's strengths was her ability to rule through her advisors and the nobility. Catherine has become infamous for rotating through confidantes as they fell out of favor. At the same time, though, effective advisors could expect great success. This is why, while traveling to view new holdings taken from the Crimean Khanate in 1787, Prince Grigory Potemkin, one of her closest aides, is said to have ordered meticulously stage-set towns built along the road, populated with well-scrubbed and well-fed peasants to laud her passing through before dismantling them and rebuilding them further along the route for her to tour again. While the tale is likely apocryphal, "Potemkin village" survives as a useful idiom for a skin-deep, sycophantic representation of a situation that covers up reality. And even though Catherine's infamous sexual dalliances are undoubtedly exaggerated, many favorites, Potemkin included, did sire children with her.

To solidify the connection between herself and Peter, the empress had a massive equestrian statue of Peter built in the center of the capital, known today as the Bronze Horseman. It is an unmissable landmark. The base is a huge stone – a glacial erratic dragged from a St. Petersburg exurb –inscribed with "Catherine the Second to Peter the First" in both Latin and Russian. Catherine saw this monument as an homage to her ancestor, even though she was only related to him through her early and ill-fated marriage.

Catherine the Great died in 1796, leaving the Russian Empire at a high point. Catherine had stepped in and implemented Peter's modernizing program to the fullest. Russia was now a full participant in European affairs and was integrated into the political, cultural, and mercantile world of the time. However, Russia finished off a glorious 18th century with one of the most darkly ironic episodes in Romanov history, a twist that undermined the Enlightenment vision of Peter and Catherine.

Catherine's son Paul was in his forties when he took the throne at his mother's passing. Ostensibly, his father was Peter III and was conceived before the latter was deposed. In portraits, he is easily recognizable by his pug-like face and upturned nose. Growing up in Catherine's shadow had made him neurotic, insecure, and paranoid. His fears were likely fed by Catherine's enemies at home and abroad who felt that a female ruler was inappropriate for fundamentally masculine, Orthodox Russia.

Once in power, Paul quickly backtracked from his mother's reforms, worried that any measure of liberty could lead to the sort of violent anti-monarchical sentiment then rocking France. He established new laws to ensure future male-only succession in the Romanov line and purged educational and government institutions of elements he saw as endangering the Tsardom. He even outlawed the use of the word "citizen," the fraternal title used by French revolutionaries.

Just like his father Peter III, Paul was obsessed with precise military displays, staying up late and getting up early to catch a glimpse of palace guard changes, marches, and drills. Even though he had neither training nor talent, Paul acted like a general, enforcing rigid obedience and strict discipline among his staff, family, and subjects. He was vindictive, petty, and vengeful. Under Catherine's advisor Potemkin, the Russian army had adopted uniforms that were both inexpensive and comfortable. They were popular with troops while also being effective and easy to produce. Paul himself redesigned the army uniforms to more closely match Prussian military fashion: expensive, rigid, and close-fitting. This seemingly simple act swiftly turned many in the military against him. Just being in his presence was tedious.

The emperor's neuroses culminated in a pervading fear of assassination by a populace infected with revolutionary fervor imported from France. Deeming the old royal palaces too dangerous, Paul designed himself a new residence, St. Michael's Castle, named after the protective archangel. The castle – a squat, ruddy-pinkish construction in a riverside Petersburg park set far from any other buildings – was surrounded by a medieval-style moat and sported flat, tall, forbidding walls. At its core was a claustrophobic courtyard. It was more fortress than palace, but Paul had at least had the foresight to place a parade ground in front of it so he could watch daily drills and reviews through the windows of his new home without even needing to leave his bed.

St. Michael's Castle, beautifully situated on the canals of St. Petersburg. Meant to be an impenetrable fortress, the castle instead saw Emperor Paul's death. Photo credit: Aleksandr Medvedkov (Dreamstime).

On a late winter's night in early 1801, after the tsar had only just moved into his castle, a small group of army officers, riled and boisterous after dinner and drinks, charged, swords drawn, into Paul's chamber. They found the tsar hiding behind curtains. In a moment, all the pent-up frustration at the tsar's insufferable meddling was loosed. Paul was dragged out from his hiding place and quickly dispatched. His youthful son, the new Emperor Alexander I, had reportedly approved the plan beforehand, but he did not actively participate. He never punished the assassins.

BY THE START of Alexander I's reign, Russia could stand confidently head-to-head with other European powers of the time. In barely a century, Russia had gone from a dark and superstitious nation to a leader in science, trade, and empire. Peter's dream had come true.

But even as Russia modernized, the rest of the world continued to shift. The 1700s brought about the birth of human rights in the modern sense – inalienable, individual, and sacred – while Russia remained unchanged in its ancient custom of serfdom and the unquestioned privileges of the monarch. And even the greatest believer in the value of autocracy had to acknowledge that, while St. Petersburg gleamed, the vast majority of Russians lived dismal rural lives in tiny villages, never traveling far from home, never learning how to read, experiencing poor medical care, and subsisting in a way that had not significantly changed in centuries. Only a small sliver of Catherine's subjects would have seen, let alone enjoyed, the changes brought about through her reforms. Adding to the mix was France's smoldering revolution. Catherine's proposal for enlightened absolutism was seemingly undercut before her death, her beloved example collapsing in breathless crowds crying out for royal blood.

The interplay between autocracy and modernization was a paradox that haunted Russia from the establishment of Peter's capital through the reign of Paul. There was no easy answer.

6

INTROSPECTION: IMPERIAL IDENTITY

Alexander I and the French | Orthodoxy, autocracy, nationality (and Decembrists) | Big in Japan | Crimea River

In the 18th century, Russia's greatest concern was becoming an integrated part of modern Europe. In the 19th, Russia reckoned with whether or not that was a good idea.

Russia struggled with how to maintain its essential Russian-ness while also jostling with international rivals, navigating this balance with mixed efficacy. This reflection began far from Russia's borders in circumstances distinctly removed from Moscow or St. Petersburg. It was sparked by two existential crises: the French Revolution and the Napoleonic Wars, which rippled through Europe in the early 19th century, and the Crimean War, which brought Russia's shortcomings into the spotlight. These flash points, given a critical eye by a rising intelligentsia, faced diagnoses that could either expose insecurities or embrace Russian exceptionalism.

BEING FAR FROM the initial fighting in Western and Central Europe, Russia was able to avoid much of the early heat of the French Revolutionary Wars, even as the tsars were shaken by the news coming out of Paris. But as the French Emperor Napoleon Bonaparte gained power, Tsar Alexander I took action to reinstate the European order. A neophyte who had only (probably) killed his father Paul four years before, he joined the Third Coalition alongside the United Kingdom and Austria to defeat France. He led his army in support of the Holy Roman Emperor's forces, but was crushed at the Battle of Austerlitz, one of Napoleon's greatest victories.[36] Russian forces withdrew, and Alexander rethought his position. Russia itself was not yet under threat, as Napoleon was more concerned with gaining ground in Central Europe, so there was breathing room.

Alexander became neutral, then joined France in an alliance via the Treaty of Tilsit in 1807. At the same time, Napoleon took control of Poland by creating the Duchy of Warsaw,

---

36. Austerlitz is sometimes called the "Battle of the Three Emperors," as it pitted Emperor Napoleon of France against Emperor Francis I of the Holy Roman Empire and Emperor Alexander I of Russia.

a client state of France. Now French territory extended east, to the Russian border. A tense peace took hold.

Napoleon suddenly turned on his ally in June 1812, mobilizing 615,000 men to march east. It was one of the largest land invasions in history up to that point. Russia's military, though of comparable size, was much less organized, experienced, and well-led than Napoleon's *Grand Armée*, which was already battle-hardened from more than a decade of successful campaigns across Europe. It was also led by the strategic master himself, Emperor Napoleon.

Napoleon easily brushed aside the initial Russian defensive lines and made a confident beeline towards Moscow. His hope was that taking this historic heart of Russia would force a quick surrender.

Tsar Alexander and his field marshal, Mikhail Kutuzov, soon realized Russia had little chance of winning on the battlefield in a direct fight. So they instead opted for attrition warfare, retreating inland while sabotaging and waylaying the French advance as much as possible. Rather than standing and fighting, Russian troops skirmished, then burned the countryside and evacuated people and goods out of the way of the French army. Thus, any town that the French encountered was already abandoned and stripped of anything useful or edible. Unable to live off the land, Napoleon's supply lines grew longer, stretching through hostile territory. Soon, with caravans coming under attack by mounted Cossack troops and dispersed Russian units, Napoleon was so far into Russian territory that to turn around was just as hazardous as to press on. With summer fading and fall approaching, he ordered his army to march faster toward Moscow, where they could hole up, consolidate, and recuperate through the winter.

Seventy miles west of Moscow, on September 7, 1812, the Russian army made a stand at the Battle of Borodino. The French narrowly carried the day, but it was a Pyrrhic victory. Crucially, Russia's defeat bought Moscow some time. Officials evacuated the city and took as much as they could with them. As the last defenders left, they opened the prisons, so the only inhabitants of the shell of a town were criminals who would compete to the death for what few provisions remained. Soon after, a fire began, started by spiteful officers or a careless ex-con. It swept through the city for four days, destroying two-thirds of Moscow and further squeezing the French ability to occupy the city.

On September 14, Napoleon entered Moscow in triumph only a few hours after the last of the Russian forces had left. The French emperor and his staff took up residence in the Kremlin. Its walls, churches, and palaces were among the few buildings still standing. The rest of the army had to make do camping among smoldering ruins.

Any relief Napoleon felt on finally reaching a large settlement that could house and feed his army quickly evaporated. The city was a picked-over, burned-out husk, with none of the provisions or shelter the French troops had hoped for – even basics like bread and firewood were either destroyed or had been evacuated. Napoleon was now deep in enemy territory with winter fast approaching. His situation was simply not sustainable, and he knew it. Already, only a third of his original force remained. Bottled up in the heart of Russia, Napoleon had

Napoleon surveys his hard-won prize in this 1841 painting by Adam Albrecht, a Bavarian painter who accompanied Napoleon on campaign and was an eyewitness to the events.

to make a choice. He could stay in Moscow and freeze, or attempt an arduous retreat back to friendly territory.

After five weeks of negotiations, in which Tsar Alexander refused to allow for peaceful transit, Napoleon chose to withdraw. The French army began its slow retreat westward on October 19. Snowflakes were already in the air.

The Russian army was quick to return to Moscow, rebuilding and fortifying it as they watched the French turn away. Russian troops continued to harass the retreating army as they trudged homeward. Starved and destitute, the French were forced to sleep outside in snowy fields dressed only in threadbare summer uniforms, eating whatever they could get their hands on. It was a dreary, cold, nerve-wracking march, not helped by random attacks by vindictive Russian horsemen. As winter continued and supplies ran even lower, Napoleon lost more men to exhaustion, starvation, and desertion than in pitched battles. He was both frustrated and embarrassed.

Napoleon clawed his way back into Polish territory in December with only 100,000 men – a fraction of what he had started with. Over half a million of Napoleon's troops had been lost in six months on the campaign, the vast majority to deaths unrelated to combat.

Marshal Kutuzov and his army continued their pursuit. Russian forces joined their allies in the Battle of Paris in 1814, occupying the city with foreign allies. According to some, Russian troops in the city left a unique cultural contribution. Hungry Russian soldiers often burst into French cafes, requesting vittles by yelling "*bystro*," the Russian word for "quickly." This may have led to the Parisian establishment of fast, food-centric cafes: bistros.

Napoleon was exiled to Elba, and Russian troops returned home. For Alexander I, the war was over. It had been a success, but one bearing a heavy cost.

In Russia, as elsewhere, Napoleon's invasion touched all aspects of life. Over one million civilians were conscripted to meet the empire's need for defense. The typical term for a conscript was a period of 25 years, a quarter-century of deadly firefights, rampaging disease, and extreme exposure to the elements. The common soldier had about a 50-50 chance of ever returning home again. Those entering the service marked their final days as if they were never to return, and few did. Sometimes, conscripts debilitated themselves to prevent service by pulling out their front teeth so that they could not tear open cartridges or by cutting off their trigger finger so that they could not fire a musket. On the home front, many saw their farms or towns destroyed, often by friendly troops to prevent them falling into French hands. Millions were displaced, families uprooted and torn apart. The Napoleonic Wars left deep scars, physically and emotionally, on nearly everyone in Russia. The conflict seared itself into national memory.[37]

Still, Russia had every right to celebrate its victory. It had conducted itself nobly in the defense of its homeland and its contributions to reinstating European peace after years of Napoleonic hooliganism. It had played its part in Napoleon's defeat; it was a battlefield partner to all the major European nations. Moscow gained an opportunity to undergo extensive urban renewal, as much of the city, destroyed by fire and occupation, was rebuilt in the latest architectural style, with wide promenades and public parks, similar to those in St. Petersburg. A massive new white-marble church with pointed domes was constructed in the center of Moscow, christened the Cathedral of Christ the Savior, to commemorate God's providence in saving Russia. In St. Petersburg, a new, neoclassical, European-inspired building, the Kazan Cathedral, was dedicated as a war memorial, and Kutuzov was interred there on his death. When Russian composer Peter Ilyich Tchaikovsky wrote the "1812 Overture" in 1882, marking seventy years from the Battle of Borodino, he used cannons as massive percussion instruments, firing them inside the concert hall to primeval, thrilling effect.[38]

In short, Russia emerged from the Napoleonic Wars renewed and confident.

PERHAPS MOST SIGNIFICANTLY, Tsar Alexander I's image of himself changed in the wake of Napoleon's defeat. He had come into his own overseeing the largest and bloodiest conflict Russia had yet experienced, and he emerged as a different person than he had entered.

---

37. For an overview of the Napoleonic Wars and its impact on Russia and the rest of Europe, see Rapport, *The Napoleonic Wars*.

38. Many July 4 fireworks celebrations in the U.S. use Tchaikovsky's celebratory work as accompaniment. This is something of a historical irony: America's struggle for independence (based on republicanism and revolution, ideals anathema to Russian autocracy) would likely have failed without French support.

As a young emperor, Alexander had largely ignored the church and looked to be on a liberalizing course. He had plans drawn up to institute a semi-democratic state legislature and meant to address the status of serfs. In 1818, he even explored the possibility of instituting a British-style constitution, and he granted Russia's new Polish holdings a high degree of autonomy and a liberal constitution. These changes seemed feasible for Russia, even overdue, and they filled young nobles and idealists with hope as Alexander appeared eager for reform.

Yet, by the early 1820s, the tsar's views had shifted in light of the revolutionary liberalism unleashed by the French Revolution. Napoleon's rise and barbaric sweep through Europe, it seemed, had started because of disgruntled peasants and overeducated, ambitious, utopian

In this full-length 1826 portrait of Alexander I by George Dawe, he wears military garb, echoing his accomplishment of defending his empire from Napoleon's invasion.

reformers. What began as a cry for reasonable, measured change had turned into guillotine executions and smoldering battlefields – excesses of irrationality, a wholesale abandonment of traditional morals. When the people were unconstrained, as the last bloody years proved, power could unravel violently.

And so, not long after defeating the French and returning to Russia, Alexander took a conservative turn. He saw himself, as well the absolute monarchs he had fought alongside in Austria and Prussia, as defenders of Christian holiness, autocracy, and order, saviors instated by God to preserve peace in the face of secular, liberal, chaos-raising reformers drunk on half-baked Enlightenment theories of democracy and human rights. The echoes of Alexander Nevsky, Dmitri Donskoy, and Minin and Pozharsky hummed in his ears to defend Russia's holy duty and carry on its sacred mantle. Alexander fell into the same thinking as previous Russian rulers. Plans for change were discarded, and control over Poland was tightened. Reforms would have to wait.

As Alexander grew even older, he became increasingly pious, enforcing conservative order throughout his land, suspicious of liberal plots to depose him and install democratic government, as had happened to French royalty. He worked closely with the Russian Orthodox Church to maintain Russian values that would support his rule. At the same time, his widespread popularity, fed by his victory, bolstered a self-conception of sacred Tsardom. Alexander was lauded as having saved Russia from French destruction and was feted around the empire.

But some in Russia were unhappy that the hero Alexander I had not been the reformer they had hoped for. When the tsar died in December 1825 without a son, cracks appeared. Many in St. Petersburg looked forward to the enthronement of his brother Constantine, the heir apparent who promised to be humane and forward-looking, if not outright progressive. He was rumored to have plans to implement a constitutional monarchy that would grant extensive rights to commoners while maintaining Russia's untouchable Romanovs.

Among Constantine's supporters were many soldiers, especially educated officers, who were veterans of the Napoleonic Wars. During their service abroad, conscripts had seen firsthand the political cultures of the Western world. They had come into contact with fellow soldiers from France, Britain, Prussia, and Austria and learned more about modern Europe than many of their countrymen. Could the economic opportunity, vibrant civil society, and crusading forward-thinking present in Western Europe be brought to Russia? As emperor, Constantine could usher in a new, more liberal Russia, one that was more in line with its neighbors, that actually implemented the humanist ideals Catherine II and Peter I had only nodded to. Some regiments were quick to swear allegiance to Constantine I, Emperor of Russia, even as officials debated who should next take up the throne.

Unfortunately, Constantine declined the crown. Instead, he chose to act as overlord of Poland, where he oversaw the further erosion of Polish liberty. His younger brother, Nicholas, took the throne instead.

A few days after Nicholas I's emperorship was announced, on the frosty morning of December 26, 1825, about 3,000 troops loyal to Constantine, mostly palace guard regiments, grenadiers, and other elite units and their officers, assembled on Senate Square in St. Petersburg, not far from the snow-covered Winter Palace and the site of the Bronze Horseman. They proclaimed their refusal to support Nicholas. The dissenters were soon met by nine thousand loyal soldiers, plus cavalry and artillery from the new tsar, deployed to disperse them, peacefully if possible.

A tense standoff ensued. Finally, after hours standing in the St. Petersburg winter, the order was given to end the demonstration by any means. Three cannons fired grapeshot into the crowd. The surviving pro-Constantine troops broke ranks, and tsarist soldiers arrested many. Some key organizers were hung for treason. Others were sent as political prisoners to Siberia, where they helped settle the wilderness in growing towns and outposts. The crackdown has been remembered as the Decembrist Revolt, and the participants and sympathizers labeled Decemberists.

Tsar Nicholas I thus began his reign with a clear message: he would not tolerate defiance.

WITH THE WAR over and new ideas flooding in after France's defeat, there were lessons to be learned and the freedom to study them. An explosion of education was bolstered by the scientific and philosophical expertise that Catherine the Great had encouraged, which had created a new class of intelligentsia. But schools under Nicholas I chiefly served the purposes of the state, and the tsar did not hesitate to use institutions to achieve unity among his subjects.

A new national ideology, as well as the foundation of a unifying identity and artistic-cultural heritage, would correct any liberal leanings. Tsar Nicholas and his advisors formulated a new slogan for the Russian state and its people: "Orthodoxy, autocracy, nationality." These three words became the foundation of a framework that permeated Russian education, history, and policy. Orthodoxy meant the ordered gathering of the holy Russian Empire under the banner of a single, supreme religion, which it was the God-appointed tsar's duty to model for his subjects. Autocracy pointed to the legal supremacy of the individual tsar, unlimited by any legal apparatus. And nationality invoked an all-encompassing unity of the Russian people that transcended ethnicity, proud and ready to defend their homeland at a moment's notice. The three intertwined and complementary ideas became the pillars of the Russian state for years to come, and have even seen a resurgence in modern, post-Soviet Russia. Even now, Putin's critics often describe the president's activities as seeking to reinstate this triad.[39]

Nicholas's new state ideology led to a high level of repression. The tsar saw himself as a general leading a vast army, ordained by God himself to achieve great aims through the obedience of his subjects. Deviation from the tsar's commands could not be allowed. Following revolutions in Europe in 1848, Nicholas banned the study of philosophy in universities altogether, and

---

39. Caro, "Vladimir Putin's 'Orthodoxy, Autocracy, and Nationality.'"

The Decembrists clash with their fellow soldiers, December 1825. The Bronze Horseman, Catherine II's monument to Peter I, is in the center-right midground. Painting by Karl Kollmann, 1830s.

officials reputedly censored letters signed "with all my love" because they implied love was withheld from God and His agent on Earth, the tsar.[40]

But not all bought into "Orthodoxy, autocracy, nationality." This was an intrinsically conservative way of conceptualizing Russia, and, as the Decembrist Revolt had demonstrated, there were plenty who disagreed. Among educated society, a divide arose that came to be emblematic of the struggle to define Russia's place in the world in the 19th century and beyond: "Slavophiles" versus "Westernizers."[41]

Slavophiles were typically more conservative. They usually believed in the exceptionalism of the Slavic peoples, especially Russia, and in Russia's claim as the Third Rome. In their lens, the tsar's dictatorial hand was a necessity of him being God's representative on earth at the helm of a holy Russian state that now carried the heavy mantle of Orthodoxy. To adopt Western-style democracy would be to forfeit this sacred inheritance and welcome godless revolutionary chaos.

The Westernizers were more liberal, seeing modernization as necessary to Russia's continued survival. Authoritarianism was a medieval anachronism, they argued, and if Russia wanted to play a major role on the world stage, it needed to adopt the humanist institutions its

---

40. Billington, *The Icon and the Axe*, 303, 380.

41. For an overview of the Slavophile-Westernizer debate, see Robinson, *Russian Conservatism*, 59-74.

Western peers had started to experiment with. Failure to do so could mean the wholesale end of the Russian state as it was left behind, unable to hold its own on the world stage.

These two competing views were extremes on a spectrum, and most stood somewhere in the middle rather than neatly in one of the two camps. This included tsars, like Nicholas I, who, for all his "Orthodoxy, autocracy, and nationality," instituted reforms to protect serfs from their masters, moving the needle slightly towards liberation while still falling short of outright freedom. More significantly, though, the Slavophile-Westernizer debate represented the crystallization of the question that had continued to come up since Peter I's time: Should Russia emulate its Western neighbors through modernization, and, if so, to what extent?

The foundation laid by the Slavophile-Westernizer debate led to an intellectual tug-of-war, as Russia's later 19th-century rulers alternated between intrinsically Russian conservative insularity and Western-style liberal reform.

Russia's post-Napoleonic self-reckoning extended to other fields as well. Cultivated by state support, prolonged peace, and educational institutions with the expertise and resources to support long-term projects, scholars began to record and preserve the culture of the Russian people. What the Brothers Grimm did for Germany, Alexander Afanasiev did for Russia, tracking down local legends and fables to create a specifically Russian collection of folk stories. "Kalinka," a supposedly timeless song about cherry trees, was first written down in 1860 and is now easily recognizable as a classic Russian folk tune. The tale of the Novgorodian merchant Sadko, a gifted musician who must outsmart wicked rulers to win treasure and a wife, was finally put to paper. Medieval stories of Russian knights, called *bogatyrs*, created much of our modern mythos around the Eastern European Middle Ages. It was at this time, too, that the first history textbooks were published by the St. Petersburg administration, putting forth a unified and purposeful history for the first time, ripe for students' consumption. This celebration of indigenous cultural achievements served a nationalistic purpose compatible with Alexander's and Nicholas's patriotic worldviews. Each folk song, each romanticized mythological painting, each fairy tale, encouraged pride in one's own nation-kin and, thereby, support for the tsar. Here was the birth of Russian patriotism.

The early 19th century also saw the rise of Russia's first well-known authors, including Alexander Pushkin and Nikolai Gogol. Of the two, Pushkin is the better remembered in Russia. He is the foundational national bard that every schoolchild reads and memorizes. By contrast, Gogol's work is edgy, surreal, and at times even absurd.

Alexander Pushkin was born to a landowning family of low nobility who lived in western Russia near the town of Pskov. His great-grandfather was a man of Central African heritage who had served Peter the Great under the name "Gannibal" (Hannibal), and his family maintained close ties to the Romanovs. Alexander was educated at a palace lyceum outside St. Petersburg.

Pushkin's writings fall squarely into the European romantic movement. His poems, short stories, and books are pastoral, emotional, and fairy-tale-like, stuffed with provincial romances,

Two of Russia's classic authors: Alexander Pushkin, left, and Nikolai Gogol, right.

noble affairs, and tragic separations. For instance, the short story "The Blizzard" follows a young woman through a mysterious winter-night wedding and a battlefield death to a fated and tidy denouement. Pushkin's poems were remarkable as well: "The Bronze Horseman" imagined Peter's statue galloping through St. Petersburg streets in a moody twilight, and his novel *Eugene Onegin* is made up of 100 14-line sonnets and tells a melodramatic story of aristocratic ennui, love, and a duel.

Pushkin's works addressed universal human emotions and social responsibility but rarely pushed the envelope. For this reason, he is little known outside of Russia. Yet this simplifies Pushkin the man: after the Decembrist revolt, Pushkin expressed sympathy for the dissenters and became a persona non grata in the capital. In 1836, the author died in a fittingly romantic way: in a duel over a scandalous love affair.

More striking is the writing of Nikolai Gogol, active from the 1830s until his death in 1852. Gogol was born in what is now Ukraine to a family of minor Cossack gentry. Gogol's work, mostly novels and short stories, is by turns dark, biting, and humorous. While he supported tsarism and was a patriot and Slavophile, he found a good deal of fodder for his work in the frivolous and officious middle-class St. Petersburg civil servants that arose around his lifetime. His point of view reflected that of many common Russians: while the tsar was a fatherly overseer who sympathized with his subjects, an army of faceless, self-important, and apathetic bureaucrats prevented any intervention that might improve the peasant's lot.

Gogol's "The Nose" sees a St. Petersburg administrator's nose jump off his face one day and assume his role at a government office, doing the worker's job as competently as he had. In the humorous ghost story "The Overcoat," a low-paid and impoverished clerk saves for months to buy a new overcoat, and his life instantly improves thanks to it. Almost immediately, though, he is mugged late at night, and his precious overcoat is taken. He soon dies, and his spirit wanders the streets of St. Petersburg ever after, in turn taking innocent people's coats from them.

While these stories are bleak, tragicomic, and creative in a way that is uniquely Russian, two of Gogol's works truly stand out as undisputed classics. "The Government Inspector" lampoons self-assured provincial bureaucrats, portraying a small-town mayor as a bumbling fool. Most subversive and enduring is Gogol's later work, *Dead Souls*. In it, a young businessman, Chichikov, seeks to make a fortune through an ingenious and creative scheme by purchasing the deeds to dead serfs for a small fee, thereby taking a tax burden off nobles' hands. Dead Souls is not only a mockery of the archaic feudal system in imperial Russia and a humorous poke at bureaucratic rigidity and self-promoting entrepreneurs; it also stereotypes Russian landowners. Who, asks Gogol, are the dead souls: the unfortunate serfs, or the frittering nobles?

Gogol's humorous satires and ridiculous plots were far ahead of their time, and, unlike the more notorious stars of Russian literature, his work is readable and relatively brief.

Following the Napoleonic Wars, Russian literature began to find its legs and its own voice, one that grappled with intrinsically Russian themes. Both Gogol and Pushkin were products of their time, defined by life under the early-19th-century tsars, Alexander I and Nicholas I.

TSAR NICHOLAS WAS an imperialist, and an imperialist in a distinctly 19th-century European sense. Throughout his reign from 1825 to 1855, Nicholas led Russia towards truly global ambitions, expanding its territory further into Eastern Europe, the Caucasus, Central Asia, and Siberia, integrating locals into a broader Russian-Eurasian cultural milieu and replacing indigenous languages and culture with national Russian-ness propagated through his trifocal lens of "Orthodoxy, autocracy, nationality." Wars to conquer and placate rebelling locals were near-constant in Georgia, Poland, the Caucasus, and Central Asia.

Further, under Nicholas, Russia enjoyed a sizable colonial empire in the Americas as Russian explorers reached the Pacific coast in Asia and continued east and south.[42] Small settlements overseen by Russian governors dotted the coast from what is now Alaska to Northern California, capturing sea otter and beaver furs to export to China and Europe. These were never as well-populated or lucrative as the colonies of other powers at the time, and were usually mere outposts where Russians were far outnumbered by local contractors of indigenous or Spanish descent, but they did add significant imperial cachet. When the fur trade dried up, many posts were simply abandoned. Russia sold their more-settled Alaskan holdings to the U.S. in 1867 for $7.2 million – $133 million today, a mere $0.37 per acre.

---

42. With mixed success, it should be noted. While exploring for Russia in the North Pacific, Vitus Bering, a Danish-born explorer for whom the Bering Strait is named, died miserably, along with much of his crew, on a remote and frigid Alaskan island in 1741. Bering's body was found years later. He was half-buried in beach sand, apparently a last-ditch effort to keep warm.

A pair of contemporary Japanese prints show Admiral Putyatin, left, and the Pallada, right.

As patriotic as Russian colonialists may have been, they also were not afraid to leverage the strengths of their rivals to their advantage. In 1852, Nicholas I dispatched Admiral Yevfimy Putyatin with the 52-gun frigate Pallada and two support ships to open up frustratingly insular Japanese markets to Russian traders.[43] The Pallada shadowed the famous American expedition charged with a similar task under Commodore Matthew Perry, and the Russians saw an opportunity to slip in once the Americans had done the talking and warmed the Japanese up. The voyage took four years and was a diplomatic success.

On board was the author Ivan Goncharov, who kept a careful journal throughout the trip. Published in 1858 as *The Frigate "Pallada,"* his account took countless Russians along on the journey. It assured them that the Russian way of imperialism, which Goncharov had seen firsthand in Siberia when returning home overland, was far superior to that he had witnessed en route, first in theory in London and then as practiced in South Africa. The voyage was a delightfully patriotic PR coup for the tsar's government.[44]

Yet Russian ambition abroad, exceptional as it might have been, led to conflict in the Balkans and Middle East as competition led to friction with other colonial powers. These tensions sparked the Crimean War, fought from 1853 to 1856.

---

43. The definitive history of the voyage can be read in Bojanowska, *A World of Empires*. See also Edwards, "The Forgotten Voyage of the Frigate *Pallada*."

44. One of Putyatin's naval officers was the brother of famous composer Nikolai Rimsky-Korsakov. While scouting the West Pacific, Voin Rimsky-Korsakov had an archipelago named after him, a title it bears to this day.

As the Ottoman Empire, the ancient Muslim archnemesis of sacred Russia, began to crumble, St. Petersburg saw an opportunity to capture some of its territory. Perhaps it was time, some thought, for Russia to take Constantinople, its fated inheritance. But major world powers, specifically Britain and France, had other ideas. They were wary of allowing Russia into the power vacuum.

Fighting began in the Balkans, but Ottoman forces, bolstered by French and British manpower, supplies, and technology, quickly pushed back Russian armies. Then the allies took the fight to Russia, landing on the Crimean Peninsula with the goal of taking the major naval base at Sevastopol, where Russia based its Mediterranean and Black Sea fleet. For nearly a year, poor leadership ordered allied forces to man siege lines, dig emplacements, and muddle through trenches, unnecessarily delaying a decisive attack. In Crimea's rugged and undeveloped terrain, troops had no choice but to camp outside. In the frigid winter, allied troops used wool full-face coverings sent from home to keep warm, naming them after their main local resupply port: Balaklava. The British and French navies blockaded Sevastopol, preventing Russian ships from escaping or relieving the defenders, but many of the besieged enjoyed more comfortable living than the allies.[45]

In September 1855, after almost a year of bombardment and starvation, Russian troops left the city quietly, surrendering it to the allies. By that point, all parties were exhausted. British and French supply and hospital lines stretched from Crimea through Istanbul and across the Mediterranean, and troops were suffering heavy casualties to firefights, exposure, and sickness. The Russian treasury and reserve of manpower were both dwindling. A peace was signed in early 1856, and the allies withdrew, leaving Crimea devastated but still in Russian hands.

Despite an inconclusive end, Russia was humiliated. The lessons Russia took from the war were sobering. Even though Russians were fighting on home turf with every advantage, their enemies had given them a run for their money. Battles between equal forces had almost universally ended in Russian defeats. If the allies had attacked Sevastopol immediately instead of trying to besiege it, the city probably would have fallen right away, opening up the vulnerable Russian mainland to conquest.

It was apparent that Russian drill, artillery equipment, and rifle technology lagged behind their French and British counterparts. The Russian navy had floundered, too: most of the fleet were either stuck in port due to the blockade or sunk quickly when engaged. One small British-French navy expedition even made it within sight of St. Petersburg, destroying oceanside forts along the way. In addition, it was obvious that the Russian economy would not be able to keep up with the wartime production that Western industrial economies found possible; as the war continued it became increasingly difficult for Russia to replace equipment destroyed in battle.

---

45. A young Leo Tolstoy, who would go on to write Russian literary classics like *Anna Karenina* and *War and Peace*, was an officer during the siege. He later wrote a memoir on his time, which he recalled fondly, punctuated with piano concerts and other refined cultural amusements as the brutal siege continued outside.

The siege of Sevastopol, an embarrassment for all involved, in a contemporary woodcut.

These concerns raised serious doubts in St. Petersburg. The invincibility of the Russian Empire was thrown into question, its methods and strategies second-guessed. Was Russia still the modern great power Catherine II had made it, the military strongman that had defeated Napoleon and turned back the dreaded Tatars? Or had the Decembrists, on that winter day in 1825, foreseen the danger of Nicholas's reign before it started? Was Russia still exceptional?

By the middle of the 19th century, Russia was the largest exporter of grain in the world. Russia's size and might made it the major power in Central Asia, Eastern Europe, and even parts of the Middle East. And its scientific and cultural achievements placed it alongside any Western peer. On the other hand, though, Russia lagged behind in heavy industry and rail transportation, which were becoming more and more critical to the exercise of state power. The economy was still largely agrarian and its transportation networks relied on rivers and unpaved roads. Farming methods, though improving, were inefficient by modern, Western standards, and the urbanizing trends and domestic consumerist class fostered by the Industrial Revolution had, as yet, failed to materialize. Almost half of Russia's population were serfs, personal property of nobles or the tsar himself. In addition, as some nations adopted early social benefits and education policies that led to higher standards of living and growing literacy even among the poor, in Russia, especially outside urban centers, these hallmarks of modernity were almost completely absent. Russian defeats on the battlefield had brought all these shortcomings into the public eye.

THE CRIMEAN WAR made it clear: the Russian Empire had chinks in its armor in nearly every respect, and this made those hiding behind it nervous.

Nicholas I died in early 1855 from pneumonia, for which he had refused treatment. The Crimean War had drained him, and he was unable to see it to its conclusion. His eldest son, Alexander II, in his late thirties, assumed the throne. After three decades under a conservative and reactionary autocrat, Russians must have wondered whether their new emperor would continue with more of the same, or present solutions to the problems that were so consistently and seriously wracking Russian society, the problems that the Crimean War had highlighted.

7

ADAPTATION: REFORMS AND COUNTER-REFORMS
A millennium of Russia | Struggles with serfdom | Alexanders II and III
| A defeat and a triumph

In 1862, the small riverside town of Novgorod was inundated with guests.

What had once been a bustling merchant republic along the Volkhov, the most prosperous and cultured city in Russia, was now a sleepy provincial center one-third of the way between St. Petersburg and Moscow. Aside from its historical attractions, it was largely indistinguishable from the hundreds of other small settlements dotting Russia's countryside. The Volkhov still carried barges on their way to St. Petersburg, and a major dirt road cut through the town, but the first railway between Moscow and St. Petersburg, opened in 1851, bypassed it. It was a quiet locale, with crumbling medieval churches scattered between modern houses and local government offices, like a setting from a pastoral Gogol story. And yet, for a few days, top Orthodox church officials, ministry heads, and even the tsar and his family made Novgorod their home. The occasion was a massive ceremony to unveil the most expensive monument built in Russia up to that time.

The Millenium of Russia Monument still stands in the center of Novgorod's kremlin, across from the ancient St. Sophia Cathedral. Its location places it at the very heart of early Russian heritage. Designed and built with the blessing of Tsar Alexander II, it marked one thousand years of the Russian state, beginning with the arrival of Russia's founding Viking warlord, Rurik, not far away.

Even today, the monument is a sight to behold, made up of over a hundred tons of bronze and towering over 50 feet high. It is massive, squat, and garish, indulgently Russian in almost every respect, shaped like a massive monarchical orb atop a plinth and covered with 127 detailed individual figures from throughout Russian history. At the top, a cross-bearing angel crowns a personification of the Russian nation, who in turn holds a shield bearing the Byzantine double-headed eagle. Around the base of the orb are sculpted full-body representations of all the personalities that contributed to the building of Russia. On one side stands an austere and warlike Rurik, and facing the other direction strides an angel-flanked Peter the Great, pushing determinedly forward towards a bright Russian future. Around the diameter of the

Tsar Alexander II, courtiers, and church officials christen the Millennium of Russia monument in Novgorod, 1862. A contemporaneous postcard.

orb, scenes from the lives of Mikhail Romanov, Ivan IV, Vladimir the Great, Boris Godunov, and others are meticulously recreated, their forms in lifelike, dynamic poses, as if frozen in place. Less memorable characters make up the level below that in bas relief. Its meticulous detail is intoxicating, disorienting, immersing, riveting. The history the monument presents is all these things, yet also a cohesive story forged into a cohesive construction.

The attendees of the unveiling ceremony must have wondered at the monument, studying the historical figures' faces and letting their eyes pick out the details of drawn swords, flowing chain mail, and extended crucifixes. They must have looked at Peter the Great, Yaroslav, and Minin and Pozharsky and wondered what lay in the future.

No doubt Tsar Alexander II glanced at his ancestors and daydreamed how he would fit into the story these predecessors had begun.

While the new Millennium of Russia monument was unapologetic, Russia as a whole lacked the same confidence. Following the Crimean War, Russia's paradoxical existence was on full display. How did Russia, a terrifyingly wealthy, massive, populated, advanced, developed, European nation, barely scrape through a war on its own land in which its enemy bungled at every turn? Russia's crisis of self-identity reached a pinnacle. Neither the Slavophiles nor Westernizers were vindicated; Russia was caught somewhere in between, paralyzed.

Something had to be done. Just what the solution was, though, would be a source of debates at all levels of Russian society for decades. For much of the later 19th and the earliest parts of the 20th century, Russia vacillated between halting progress and stubborn reactionism.

IF ALEXANDER II did feel historical weight on his shoulders, he acted on it decisively. From a young age, Alexander II broke from the conservative Romanov strain that had characterized the reigns of Alexander I and Nicholas I. Feeling pressure from the populace, if not from the aristocracy, Alexander, soon after his coronation in 1855 and not long before christening Novgorod's monument to celebrate one thousand years of Russian history, embarked on a series of reforms that turned Russian society upside down. While not outright abandoning his father's notion of "Orthodoxy, autocracy, nationality," Alexander II both saw the need to update Russian policies and had the will to do so. Because of this, his reign represents a turning point in imperial Russian history.

Alexander II's most notable reform was the emancipation of the serfs, ending an institution that had been an inextricable part of Russia for centuries. Since long before the Romanovs, nobles had worked their lands by using human property. Nobles might own entire towns, with serfs of various trades and skills, all overseen by the landowner himself. Serfs enjoyed few personal rights, and yet were still required to pay taxes and fulfill draft duties; they had all the responsibilities of citizenship with none of the benefits. While the population of serfs as a proportion of the Russian population had declined steadily over the previous century, millions were still serfs, owned either by landowners or the state. With debates about slavery raging abroad, serfdom, the effective enslavement of one's own people, became more and more an obvious anachronism.

When the tsar enacted the first laws that led to the abolition of serfdom in 1861, nobles had two years to free their serfs and give them part of their farms. Still, as a compromise for dismantling the rural economy, the new laws favored landowners, who usually kept the most fertile parts of their land for themselves and received compensation for their lost income. The newly-freed serfs, with little resources of their own, were forced to cultivate less lucrative areas and were often conned out of sustainable wages and prices. Some simply stayed working at the same estates, but for meager pay and while receiving none of the protection and emergency supplies they had once received from their owners. Many left for large cities to join Russia's small, though growing, manufacturing industries.

In addition to freeing the serfs, Alexander II also set in motion a set of judicial reforms aimed at making the legal system more equitable for those of all classes. Village communes, or zemstvos, would now have a standardized system for leveraging economic and political power, which answered to centralized Russian authority. This gave peasants, poor as they were, an institution where they could be monitored by the St. Petersburg bureaucracy while also offering them a means to effect grassroots change.

Further, Alexander II founded new universities and encouraged education, reversing the cooling effect of his predecessor. Many German professors made their way to Russia, bringing with them new political and philosophical ideas and reinvigorating the intelligentsia. And the tsar supported the construction of new industries and railroads, bringing in British,

French, and American engineers to build a new transit network to tie together his sprawling domain.

The tsar's relatively lax restrictions on censorship, though still far from a free press, allowed for the refinement of Russian art. This included the work of two of Russia's most famous authors: Dostoevsky and Tolstoy. Their influence tints all Russian literature, for better or worse.

Fyodor Dostoevsky's life was plagued by poverty, gambling, and alcohol abuse, and he often found himself in serious debt, even after he won critical acclaim and widespread popularity. In his youth, under Nicholas I, his involvement in a group that circulated banned books got him arrested and sentenced to execution. As he stood before the firing line, hooded and about to face death, a messenger from the tsar arrived, relating that his sentence had been lightened to four years in Siberian exile.

As an adult, Dostoevsky became staunchly pious and deeply conservative. Readers might be surprised to find that, rather than the radical liberalism and anti-establishment freedom many dissident authors espouse, Dostoevsky's work leans more towards tradition and Orthodox Christian discipline. He was chiefly concerned with moving "from the real to the more real," that is, from the place of materialist reality to the transcendent human reality of relationships, ideas, and the soul.[46] For instance, his best-known book, *Crime and Punishment*, is an indictment of nihilistic secularism, painting it as morally corrupt. It instead upholds a principle of universal morality that cannot be twisted by modern rationalism. Likewise, *The Brothers Karamazov* and *The Idiot* deal with themes of faith, family, and the meaning of suffering and sin. To Dostoyevsky, the liberal thinkers fuelled by industrial rationalism could answer the questions of science and economic prosperity, but not the more important questions of human purpose and day-to-day morality. His nuanced philosophical undercurrent, hashed out by deep characters through rich dialogue, is one of the reasons why his work is so infamously impenetrable for modern audiences. The ideology Dostoevsky lands on is not quite pro-tsar patriotism; instead, it might be most accurate to say that he was an Orthodox Christian humanist-anarchist.

And then there is Tolstoy. Leo Tolstoy self-described his works as "not quite novels." Instead, they are sprawling works of aristocratic family drama rooted in history. For instance, his magnum opus, *War and Peace*, traces five families through the fallout of the Napoleonic Wars. Similarly, *Anna Karenina* follows the socially scandalous noble dalliances of the title character. In the famous words of Karenina's opening paragraph: "Happy families are all alike; every unhappy family is unhappy in its own way," unleashing from the start high-society family angst and characters full of conflicting motivations and loyalties searching for meaning. Both of Tolstoy's most famous works are around a thousand pages long and are richly populated with unique characters and striking settings.

---

46. Billington, *The Icon and the Axe*, 416.

Remarkably, after the success of *Anna Karenina*, Tolstoy became a religious teacher with a large following. Like Dostoevsky, he hewed to Russia's traditional Orthodoxy, but with a more populist flair. He admired the peasantry for their simplicity and proclaimed a puritanical message for finding meaning in life. He grew out his beard, became vegetarian, and wore traditional garb. Tolstoy died anonymously in a rural train station at age 82. Depending on who you ask, he was either traveling to proclaim his philosophy to the masses or trying to escape from the suffocating influence of his family.

Music also thrived under Alexander II. Pyotr Ilyich Tchaikovsky is instantly recognizable from his 1812 Overture and ballets like *The Nutcracker* and *Swan Lake*. Likewise, Nikolai Rimsky-Korsakov, composer of *Scheherezade*, was a master of orchestral music. These composers and their colleagues solidified Russia's identity as a leader in the classical musical world, its musicians playing in the finest concert halls in Italy, France, and the United States. It was also at this time that famous ballet and musical theaters throughout Russia began to open and cater to refined tastes with both indigenous and foreign performances, like the Mariinsky in St. Petersburg and the Bolshoi in Moscow.

The cultural explosion ushered in by Alexander II's progressive approach opened the door for further development later. By the early 1900s, Ilya Repin had become the major painter of Russian historical and cultural scenes, and Anton Chekhov's short stories and plays had gained a worldwide audience with their quick wit and punchy writing that grappled with themes of progress and quiet tragedy. Even some experimentation into modern expressions began to appear in the form of Alexander Scriabin, who reconceptualized musical tones to create unearthly melodies, and Vasily Kandinsky, whose abstract artworks uncannily communicated movement on a still canvas. Perhaps most famously, Igor Stravinsky's ballet *The Rite of Spring* outraged (and then later wowed) Parisian audiences when it debuted in 1913, with its dissonant music and jarring, primitive choreography.

Yet these developments were, in a sense, reserved for the elite. Those who rose to prominence in the arts – musical, visual, or literary – were almost solely from the burgeoning middle class or still higher social tiers. These were men whose parents could afford to send them to school to unlock their talents and bankroll their passions. What did Dostoevsky or Repin or Tchaikovsky mean for someone in a remote village of the Russian Empire, someone who had never set foot in a large town, let alone St. Petersburg or Moscow? Probably very little.

And there was a darker side to legal reforms and artistic progress. Alexander II's new freedoms released a genie that was tough to put back in the bottle. The thousands of newly-freed peasants flocking to cities created social tension and economic upheaval as they searched for new direction. Populations in Russian-occupied territories like Finland, Ukraine, and Poland, now more free to rediscover their national heritages, began to chafe even more against Moscow's imperial rule and the Russianization it imposed. Rebellions, like Poland's 1863 push for independence, were mercilessly crushed.

Indeed, rather than venting unrest, the loosening of censorship only worsened it. Dissident groups finally felt free to gather and publish their views. Some of these groups were radicals who had imported ideas of anarchism and socialism from the West, while others were made up of well-educated young Russians from the intellectual classes who sought a republic or limited democratic reforms.

Amid this social turmoil, Alexander II was the subject of a half-dozen assassination attempts. After the first, in 1866, Alexander II retreated from his liberalism, clearly believing that when he gave his people an inch, they took a mile, sometimes violently. He stopped short of pushing through any more radical changes, acting with deliberation and suspicion, as if his subjects had lost his trust. For the rest of his reign, Alexander only reluctantly relinquished centralized power. He fell victim to the same disillusionment that had plagued Catherine II and Alexander I.

On March 13, 1881, the tsar was in a carriage en route to the Hermitage's Winter Palace, making his way home from a military ceremony in central St. Petersburg. As the carriage cruised along one of the city's iconic canals, a bomb was lobbed under the hooves of one of the horses. It exploded, wounding the horses and killing a Cossack guardsman. The carriage halted, and Alexander exited his bulletproof compartment to investigate the carnage and check on his bodyguard. At that moment, another assassin threw a second bomb, destroying the tsar's legs. The attackers, members of an anarchist cell, were quickly accosted, but Alexander was gravely wounded. He was helped back to the Hermitage but soon died.

A cathedral was built on the site of the assassination. The Church of the Savior on Spilled Blood is a 19th-century echo of St. Basil's traditional Muscovite onion domes, but with colors and patterns that are subdued under more modern architecture. The church remains there to this day, covering the street where the anarchists struck, its footprint jutting into the canal. A miraculously still-bloody patch of cobblestones is preserved inside, under striking blue and gold mosaics of biblical scenes.

And so, Alexander II's son, Alexander III, took the throne. He was 36 and, given the circumstances that led to his father's death, strongly interested in maintaining the status quo, avoiding reform, and, in some cases, even reversing his father's efforts. For the 13 years of his rule, Alexander III was traditional and tight-fisted.

Alexander was not meant to be tsar. Only when his brother – already educated and polished to take the reins – died from disease was Alexander III thrust into the role of heir apparent, already past the age of education that would have smoothed out the rough edges of his personality. Whereas his father was cultured and refined, thoughtful and forward-looking, Alexander III embraced a Russian-flavored coarseness in both his personal and professional lives. Photographs of Alexander II show him with a prodigious, fastidiously-fashioned mustache and engaged, thoughtful eyes. Alexander III is, by comparison, heavy-set and intense, with something in his brow that suggests a hint of Rurikovich brazenness. Contemporary

Church of the Savior on Spilled Blood today, the site of Alexander II's assassination. Photo credit: Xantana (Dreamstime).

accounts describe him as swaggering with masculine assurance and confidence, rarely second-guessing himself. He was the archetypal Russian bear: hairy, brusque, manly.

Case in point: In 1888, the imperial train, carrying the royal family, exceeded a safe traveling speed and violently derailed. Twenty-three servants were killed, but all the Romanovs survived. Government staff spread the story that the tsar himself had held up the collapsed roof of the dining car to allow his family to escape unharmed.

Shortly after his coronation and already anticipating hostility from his people, Alexander moved his family from the urban Winter Palace to a more defensible, suburban royal residence. He quickly doubled down on Nicholas I's policies of "Orthodoxy, autocracy, nationality." Censorship was re-tightened. When a severe famine led to a cholera outbreak in rural areas, Alexander III's solution was to take power from the provincial zemstvos rather than empower them, a move that felt like a betrayal to rural communities. He also pursued a determined policy of Russification throughout the empire, quashing any thoughts of independence or cultural autonomy for minority groups in occupied territories. Jewish families especially saw greater restrictions, with legislation forbidding them from certain professions and dictating the Pale of Settlement in the borderlands of the empire where they were allowed to live. To enforce all these measures, Alexander formed the Okhrana, a secret police organization dedicated to covertly sniffing out underground resistance movements and bringing their members to justice before they could wreak havoc.

Russia was in the hands of a tyrant.

IN 1894, WHEN Alexander III died of kidney disease in a palace in sunny Crimea (he was only 49), his son, the 26-year-old Nicholas II, took power. Considered by his father to be effeminate, frail, and indecisive, a spoiled pretty-boy, Nicholas II enjoyed the finer parts of 19th-century royal life. He was well-educated, thoughtful, and athletic. At home, he rowed boats on palace lakes and played tennis with his family. As a young prince he had cavorted through Europe with the uppermost crust of the nobility and was well connected through both blood and friendship.[47] Nicholas was very close with his family, especially his son and German-born wife. But his personality had a callous side, too. By turns, Nicholas could project himself as genteel and kind, yet he was also prone to stubbornness, self-interest, and irrationality.

Still, perhaps Nicholas II could be the right tsar at the right time. Reforms had been started by Alexander II but stopped by Alexander III. The new tsar faced a choice: push for liberalization or ensconce himself in the traditional autocracy of the Russian tsars.

Nicholas's reign began poorly. At a massive public celebration planned to correspond with the invite-only inauguration ceremonies, a human stampede occurred, killing more than a thousand commoners and wounding many more. News was quickly relayed to Nicholas, but rather than stopping the royal festivities, he continued on, not pausing to acknowledge his convalescing and dead subjects. For this he appeared haughty, detached, and uncaring. It was a black omen for the new emperor. Shortly after, he dismissed a delegation of peasants desiring a reinstitution of the power of the zemstvos. He was not shaping up to be the reformer many hoped for.

But these faux pas were soon eclipsed by a feather in his cap. In 1899, Nicholas spearheaded a global peace conference at the Hague in the Netherlands. There, among two dozen of the world's great and minor nations, Nicholas II and Russian thought leaders helped implement a pioneering system of secular international law, setting out conventions on war crimes, treatment of prisoners, and unbreachable human rights. The conference was a world first. Between the 1899 conference and another one that Nicholas oversaw in 1907, much of our modern understanding of international law was codified. This aspect of Nicholas II's tenure is often overlooked in the West, but many Russians invoke it with pride. A third conference was scheduled for 1915, but was canceled due to the gruesome conflict now known as the First World War.

NICHOLAS FACED THE first major crisis of this rule, not from a home-grown threat, but from Russia's Far East: the Russo-Japanese War.

Russian and Japanese imperial competition in the Pacific placed the two nations on a collision course. Since the Pallada's expedition 50 years earlier, Japan had rapidly industrialized and expanded. Its next step was to gain a foothold on mainland Asia. Russian holdings were

---

47. Nicholas II reportedly looked so alike to his cousin, Britain's future King George V, that Queen Victoria had a difficult time telling them apart.

a prime target, and Russia, its population and manufacturing centers a world away, did not pose a serious threat.

Under cover of darkness, the Japanese executed a surprise torpedo boat attack on the Russian Pacific Fleet moored at Port Arthur, on the coast of modern China, on the night of February 8-9, 1904.[48] The Japanese then followed this up with a well-organized navy-backed siege. By the time Port Arthur fell, seven Russian battleships had been sunk with no Japanese losses. Troops swiftly disembarked, quickly occupying much of Russian-held Manchuria.

The Russian military was powerless to counterattack. Even once the Trans-Siberian Railroad was completed four months later, in June 1904, much of the line was single-track, severely limiting the movement of troops, supplies, and the wounded. It could take weeks, if not months, for reinforcements to arrive. And with the Pacific Fleet neutralized, Russia had to send its Baltic Sea Fleet to counter the Japanese naval threat. With battleships too large to pass through the Suez Canal, the newly rechristened Second Pacific Fleet took seven grueling months to round Africa, navigate the Indonesian Archipelago, and finally make it to the campaign theater. The trip was marred with disease, trigger-happy gunners who mistook British fishing trawlers for Japanese torpedo boats, and diplomatic tensions caused by damaged undersea cables in French African colonies. When the fleet finally arrived in the Strait of Tsushima in May 1905, the war was already effectively over. Still, the Japanese fleet engaged. In the ensuing battle, all the Russian battleships and most of their support vessels were lost to a mere three destroyed Japanese torpedo boats. The Japanese fleet had crushed the Russian flotilla with almost no losses.

Things were no better on the home front. The cost of the war strained the Russian economy to its limits, causing food shortages and price hikes that hit working-class civilians hardest. Demonstrations and strikes became increasingly common. On January 22, 1905, thousands of protesters and strikers marched towards the Winter Palace, led by a priest carrying a petition calling for relief for the poor. They came under fire from the tsar's troops, who had been sent to restore order. The state's aggressive reaction resulted in the deaths of more than a hundred, and the day has been remembered since as Bloody Sunday. Six months later, in the Black Sea, the crew of the battleship Potemkin mutinied. The sailors, mostly enlisted seamen who were dissatisfied with poor rations, rebelled against their officers and took refuge in Romania, escaping punishment.

Despite these signals, Tsar Nicholas II held out, convinced that a Russian victory was just around the corner. But by September 1905, it was clear that Japan had the upper hand and was unlikely to relinquish it anytime soon. Nicholas and the Russians were forced to give up. Representatives of the two sides met and agreed on peace terms in Portsmouth, Maine. The treaty was brokered by U.S. President Theodore Roosevelt, who received a Nobel Peace Prize

---

48. A similar tactic of sudden, preemptive strike would be adopted for the attack on the American naval base at Pearl Harbor in 1941.

Ilya Repin's impressionistic portrayal of crowds cheering the 1905 Revolution, which promised a comprehensive overhaul of Russia's government.

for his effort. Russia was forced to give up territory in the Far East and Manchuria, and Japan gained a border with China. It was another humiliating peace.

Back in St. Petersburg, Nicholas was forced to acknowledge the poor internal state of the empire, which was wracked by strikes and unrest throughout 1905. Swallowing his aversion to change, in October 1905 he released the October Manifesto, which allowed all males in the lands of the Russian Empire the right to vote for a representative body called the State Duma, which would partner with the tsar on the creation of state policy. In addition, the basic human rights of Russian civilians were formally enshrined, including freedom of religion, speech, and assembly. These reforms became known as the 1905 Revolution. The October Manifesto was the most sweeping, modernizing set of reforms the Romanovs ever implemented.

LIKE THE CRIMEAN War 50 years before, the Russo-Japanese War highlighted Russian weakness. Russia was exposed both at home and abroad. If isolated Japan, so recently an uncivilized colonial target, could not only take on but handily defeat one of Europe's most powerful players, maybe Russia was not so great after all. As had occurred in the Crimean War (and, more recently, in Ukraine), a conflict begun with confidence devolved into desperation and then emergency.

Yet the October Manifesto, a response to failure on the battlefield, brought hope and optimism. Perhaps this was finally the turning point that dissident groups had clamored for. The door was open to Russia's modernization; Alexander II's work could at last be taken up again.

Would the changes stick this time?

8

DISSOLUTION, CONFUSION, AND REVOLUTION: THE END OF THE ROMANOVS

Sputtering reform | The discontents | Rasputin and the royals | Wartime strain | Shooting tsars

The October Manifesto was not a panacea for Russia's ills. The changes of 1905 only further underscored the need for more significant reforms. Renewed calls for change culminated in the Russian Revolution of 1917 – a period of chaos, upheaval, and rapid shift. And from it sprung a novel state, a new political experiment based on a new political philosophy.

The final years of the Romanovs' 304-year reign were fraught with pressure from multiple corners. The Russian Revolution that unseated them was later embellished and made into a founding myth for a new Russia, one that served as a hagiography for its leaders. Similarly, for foreigners, the romantic, nostalgic tales of a glittering world vanishing in blood and fire cultivated interest but cast the real story into legend, obfuscating the truth. This has created a picture that is difficult to parse, with conflicting accounts twisted by rumor and crying out to be reconciled.

Yet it is fitting that the all-powerful Russian autocracy should crumble in unmanageable turmoil and disorder.[49]

WHILE THE 1905 Revolution was greeted with ecstasy, when the new democratic Duma convened in 1906, it was profoundly toothless. While any new law or decree could be recommended by the Duma, it also had to be approved by Nicholas II and the State Council, a group of advisors only Nicholas could appoint. Further, the tsar had the power to order new Duma elections at his whim, and the tsar could always pass emergency decrees without Duma approval anyway. He could even swap out the prime minister of the Duma based on his preference, with no input from the people or their representatives. In fact, only four days before the first session of the Duma on April 27, 1906, Nicholas II gave himself the title of "Supreme Autocrat."

---

49. Some indispensable sources on the Gordian knot of the final years of the Russian Empire, Russia in the First World War, and the Russian Revolution include: Florinsky, *The End of the Russian Empire*; Rappaport, *Caught in Revolution*; Sanborn, *Imperial Apocalypse*; and Smele, *The "Russian" Civil Wars*.

Nicholas II addresses the opening of the first State Duma in the Winter Palace, St. Petersburg, 1906.

Thus Nicholas clutched to his authority even as it seemed to be eroding beneath him. The Duma quickly became little more than a collection of powerless aristocrats largely supportive of the tsar, sycophants who were supposed to be representing the common man but in reality did very little. The opportunity to run for office seemed futile, so many reform-based political parties simply boycotted elections, deeming them shams and deciding instead to work outside the institution to effect change.

It was against this backdrop that one of history's largest personalities emerged: Vladimir Ilyich Ulyanov, or, as he called himself, Lenin. Lenin was the main leader of the communist front during the Russian Revolution, presenting Marxism as an alternative to the entrenched conservative autocracy. Lenin's strain of Marxism, once applied to the Russian context, dominated for some 70 years. Yet Lenin himself was a product of his time and the ideology he preached, and so some background is necessary.

Marxism is named for German journalist and political theorist Karl Marx, who formulated the ideology of communism while living in Victorian London some 50 years before Lenin's time. Seeing the Dickensian struggles of the everyday English workingman, as well as the excessive riches accumulated by wealthy industrialists, Marx proposed a novel explanation of the industrial economic system and, along with it, a way out for the poor worker. His theory posited that developed industrial societies were built through the exploitation of cheap labor (the proletariat class) by capitalist fatcats (the bourgeoisie) who prevented the workers who actually produced wealth from organizing to defend their rights and livelihoods. Eventually, Marx asserted, the divide would become unsustainable. The workers would rise up in violent revolution to take over the means of production. This would usher in a new society based on the empowerment of the poor and marginalized worker, called socialism. Before long, the "dictatorship of the proletariat" would evolve into the worker's utopia where everything would be held in common: communism.

Russia in the late 19th and early 20th century was already a hotbed for revolutionary thought. As it became increasingly apparent that the Russian state was unable and unwilling to change, its prestige waning in the modern world, different groups proposed different paths forward. Some, like the group that killed Alexander II, were anarchists, while others were radically conservative. Still others called for American-style liberalism or moderate constitutional constraints on absolutist monarchy. But the far-left perspective was particularly influential in Russia. Here was an all-powerful autocrat who hoarded power and drip-fed half-hearted reform to placate his people, enabled by self-serving nobles and a political system designed to box out commoners. Most rural working-class Russians, typically the descendants of former serfs, lacked access to basic healthcare and education. Those in the cities lived in cramped housing and toiled in factories for low pay. Abetting the system was the Russian Orthodox Church, which appeared to be keeping the masses in quiet obedience through teachings that only further served the ruling classes.

While Marx himself discounted the possibility of a communist revolution in Russia and rarely engaged with Russians (as it was far from the sort of industrial society he had built his theory on), to Lenin and others, Russia was the very picture of the corrupt capitalist society Marx described in his writings. Lenin observed Russia's political and social issues through the lens of Marx's theories and wrote widely about the need for revolution in his homeland (and elsewhere). In Lenin's eyes, tsarism, Russian Orthodoxy, and the Russian economy were real-life cases that Marx's ideas could be tested on.

Like Marx, Vladimir Ilyich Ulyanov came from a comfortably middle-class provincial family.[50] While his ancestors were freed serfs, his father was a successful university professor. Vladimir's older brother had been a member of radical student groups in the late 1800s and had been executed for an attempted assassination on Alexander III. This, coupled with his time at Kazan University, led to Vladimir's adoption of a politics infused with revolutionary and socialist strains in the early 1890s.

Young Vladimir threw himself into activity as an activist, writing and publishing a collection of tracts and books on leftist philosophy and networking with sympathetic intellectuals throughout Europe. He was charismatic and persuasive, a captivating and passionate speaker and prolific writer. When he ran afoul of the tsar, his political activities forced him into exile.

---

50. Neither were members of the proletariat class themselves.

But Ulyanov used these periods to network with left-wing organizations abroad and make a name for himself as a major figure in the European socialist-communist movement. In 1901, Vladimir Ilyich Ulyanov changed his last name to "Lenin," likely a nod to a Siberian river near where he spent time in exile.

In 1903, a schism occurred in the Russian Social Democratic Party, where Lenin and the socialist left planted their flag. The disagreement arose out of party structure and revolutionary strategy: Lenin and those who followed him favored a tightly controlled membership made up of professional activists who would force Russia into socialism, skipping the capitalist stage Marx said had to precede the revolution and that Russia had yet to experience. They called themselves "Bolsheviks," meaning "Majority," even though they were smaller than their opponents, the "Mensheviks," meaning "Minority." The Mensheviks favored more open membership and argued that Russia needed to experience bourgeois capitalism first before it would be possible to effect the revolution. When he led the split from the Social Democrats, Lenin may have alienated many of his allies on the left, but the Bolshevik Party soon drew many who were frustrated with the current system and were ready to tear it down, violently if necessary.

When the 1905 Revolution flopped, Lenin urged the Bolsheviks to take up arms and literally fight for their place in the Duma if they could not earn it fairly. But the tsar's secret police, the Okhrana, caught wind of his plans. Lenin fled to Europe, where he and his wife, Nadezhda Krupskaya, continued to write and engage with dissident groups. In Russia, the Bolsheviks joined the myriad other political organizations unleashed by the 1905 Revolution in jostling for power both inside and outside the Duma, with little success.

The Duma remained little more than a token nod to liberalism with no real power. Tsar Nicholas II and his family saw the body as an uppity group of self-righteous commoners. To have them walking around the palace was simply disgusting, a violation of the sacred residence of a holy monarch. Those at extreme ends of the spectrum, like Lenin and his ilk, who were not even represented in the Duma, were insignificant ants not even worth the effort of squashing.

And Nicholas did not hesitate to exercise his rights in the Duma, ensuring it met his own ends through personal appointments and imperial decrees. As it became obvious that the Duma was merely a vehicle for the exercise of the tsar's power, the tsar, his prime minister, and the Duma representatives came to be seen more and more as out-of-touch figureheads with little interest in the true welfare of the common people, who became jaded after the optimistic spirit of 1905 dried up. By the early 1910s, dissent and unrest were simmering just beneath the surface of the public sphere.

IN 1913, THE Romanovs celebrated the 300th anniversary of the start of their rule. Nicholas II held a lavish ball for the nobility, and the royal family retraced the route Mikhail Romanov had taken from his Kostroma monastery to Moscow after his election as tsar. Celebrations were held throughout the land year-round. Many featured cannon salvoes, parades, and performances of *A Life for the Tsar*. Nicholas and his family were the focus of it all. It was less a celebration of Russia than it was a celebration of the person of the tsar himself.

Developments in August 1914 ended any possibility of further political reform in Russia. World war brought conflict to Russia's European borderlands, and the entire country turned to the war effort.

Russia was one of the first powers to join in the melee. When Austria-Hungary threatened to invade Serbia in retaliation for the assassination of the Austrian heir, Serbian authorities called on their fellow Slavs in Russia to defend them. In response, Russia vowed to protect Serbia ferociously. From there, Austria leveraged its ally Germany, and Russia called in its allies France and Great Britain.

As elsewhere, the opening shots of the conflict were met with nationalistic passion. Many young volunteers signed up with eagerness before later becoming cynical about the enterprise. Tsar Nicholas II renamed St. Petersburg to the more-Russian "Petrograd" to distance the city from any Germanic influence that Peter I might have bestowed on it.

Tsar Nicholas II and family in 1913. Empress Alexandra stands over Nicholas's left shoulder. The famous Princess Anastasia has her arm around young Prince Alexei, the hemophiliac heir.

Decimated at first at the Battle of Tannenberg shortly after the start of the war, Russian forces soon stabilized their front line. However, as in the Russo-Japanese War, reinforcement of the front was hampered by the country's uneven development and insufficient rail lines. Military strategy hinged on where officers could find supplies for their men, placing Russia at an operational disadvantage. In addition, with a weaker industrial base, many of Russia's factories built to serve the civilian market had to shift away from their usual production to create war materiel. As a result, once again, prices on domestic goods soared. With more resources sent to the front, even bread and coal became scarce in urban areas. When winter came, the inability to get food and fuel was keenly felt.

At the same time, the royal family began to appear increasingly aloof. Already dealing with a populace losing faith in him, the tsar tried to use the war to improve his public image. Nicholas traveled to the front regularly, taking symbolic control of the armed forces in 1915 and personally encouraging his troops on the front lines. But even as Nicholas tried to show himself as a caring father to his people, his noble ideals of honorable leadership were a farce compared to the conflict's brutality. Further, the private life of Nicholas's family and rumors of juicy scandals confounded his efforts and further tarnished his reputation, eroding trust in the Romanovs wholesale.

Nicholas had five children: Olga, Tatiana, Maria, Anastasia, and Alexei. Olga was the oldest, 19 in 1915. Anastasia was the youngest girl, at 15, and Alexei, Nicholas's heir, was 11. Alexei had hemophilia, a blood disease that causes painful bruising and prevents blood from clotting. For years, Empress Alexandra took Alexei to Russia's top doctors in an effort to heal his condition and provide relief. Yet no medical professional was able to help in a meaningful way. Alexei seemed to be cursed, weak, but for this his mother and father showed special tenderness towards him.

What Russia's medical establishment failed to do, a strange man from the provinces had a knack for. Grigory Rasputin was a mystic Orthodox priest from a small village in Siberia who had moved to St. Petersburg and made a name for himself as a healer and spiritual counselor among the nobility. With piercing eyes and hypnotizing mannerisms that caught the attention of many who encountered him, Rasputin cut an iconic figure. He also had a penchant for drink and could often be found in the company of married aristocratic women.

After Rasputin made contact with the royal family, Empress Alexandra discovered that he, more than any other religious or medical professional, could soothe Alexei's pain and prevent the onset of bruises. She and her son began spending a good deal of time with Rasputin, who became, in effect, a member of the royal family when Nicholas II was off directing the war effort. While some claimed Rasputin was a charlatan, his cure a placebo, others, including Empress Alexandra, swore by his powers. Meanwhile, for common Russians who knew about the situation, it seemed as though their sons were dying ignominiously while fighting the Germans in Poland at the same time as the Romanovs were most concerned with having a good time with a drunken, lecherous holy man with an unkempt beard.

By 1916, the nobility had had enough of the Romanovs' flirting with Rasputin, whom they considered to be a low-class manipulator undermining the legitimacy of the state. On a December night, a group of noblemen lured Rasputin to one of the poshest homes in St. Petersburg, that of the Yusupov family. Saying that a group of hard-partying aristocrats were heading out to some social clubs that night, Prince Yusupov and his accomplices led Rasputin into a cellar room, where they invited him to have some poisoned tea, pastries, and wine while the rest of the group gathered. After sipping and munching the toxic vittles for an hour with no results, and with Rasputin becoming impatient to head out, one of the nobles pulled out a pistol and shot him in the chest, which seemed to kill him. The nobles tied Rasputin up as they discussed what to do with the body. But then, an hour later, Rasputin suddenly jumped up, wrestled out of his restraints, and flew out the door. As he entered the palace courtyard, one of the assassins shot Rasputin again. The holy man collapsed into a bank of snow, unmoving. Yusupov and his associates dumped Rasputin's body into the Neva River. He was found the next morning, legend has it, clinging to a bridge support, dead not from poison, drowning, or a gunshot wound, but exposure to the freezing air. Further, the story goes, as his body was cremated, it sat up, stubbornly refusing to die peacefully.[51]

The entire royal family, especially Empress Alexandra and Prince Alexei, mourned the loss of a man who had been one of their closest associates. With Rasputin gone, Alexandra's actions became more erratic as her mental health suffered. From the outside, it seemed the Romanov family was tearing itself apart.

Still the war dragged on.

AS THE ECONOMY limped through the bitter winter of 1916-17, the government had to impose rationing. This only increased discontent. Necessities were scarce. Dissenters of diverse political stripes used the frustration of the common people to bolster their numbers and swell strikes and marches. This was a gold mine for more extreme parties like the Bolsheviks: economic hardship, a drawn-out military campaign, and out-of-touch royalty all framed militant socialism as a promising alternative. Lenin continued to contribute to the party as much as he could from his exile in Switzerland.

Tensions finally came to a head in February 1917.[52] After eight days of violent street demonstrations against shortages of basic life necessities, the city garrison of Petrograd defected to the demonstrators. The Romanovs were left with few allies and even fewer options. In the

---

51. In a strange twist of fate, Rasputin's daughter Maria escaped to the United States after the Revolution and became a big cat tamer in a traveling circus, eventually settling down in Los Angeles. She had two dogs, "Yussou" and "Pov," named for the prince who killed her father. She died in America in 1977. See Edwards, "Tiger Queen."

52. Until the Revolutions of 1917, Russia was on the Julian Calendar, an older version of the modern Gregorian calendar, and as a result dates lagged two weeks behind. This is not much of an issue except in 1917. I use the Gregorian calendar dates here for the sake of consistency, as I have done throughout. The "February Revolution," when the tsarist regime fell, took place mostly in March, and the "October Revolution," when the Bolsheviks took power, was mostly in November. This has also given rise to the rumor that the Russian delegation to the Olympic Games of 1912 was two weeks late because of their calendar. There is little evidence for this from reputable sources.

midst of such pressure, and sensing the shift in the wind, on March 15, 1917, Nicholas II abdicated the throne. His 12-year-old son was offered the crown, but Alexei quickly declined it. After more than 300 years leading Russia, the Romanovs were removed from power and placed under house arrest in one of their suburban palaces.

True revolution had come to Russia at last. Demonstrators and ad hoc leaders quickly cobbled together a Provisional Government, a multiparty governing body that snatched national power from the tsar and Duma. They shared rule with the Petrograd Soviet, a local worker's association, in the former Duma chamber.

Yet things did not immediately improve. With the tsar's deposition, Russia was without a head. In Petrograd and Moscow, violence and demonstrations continued as workers called for an end to the war and better economic prospects, voicing what became their famous slogan, "Peace, land, and bread." The Provisional Government was eager to get to work, but had trouble executing power – it had little legitimacy to leverage. Its many factions, including not just the Bolsheviks and Mensheviks but also the entirety of the political spectrum, jockeyed for position, paralyzing meaningful progress. Gunfights, looting, and the destruction of property were commonplace in towns throughout Russia. Armies awaited orders in the field, even as the central government no longer existed. Countless cities and towns outside of the European core had not even participated in the Revolution, yet they now answered to a new authority.

Russia was effectively rudderless, embroiled in anarchy through much of early 1917.

Through all this, Lenin was stuck in Switzerland, isolated amid a war-torn Europe. However, the Central Powers were interested in ending the war with Russia so that they could fully focus on the Western Front. As a way to hamstring their enemy, the German government agreed to shuttle Lenin, his wife, and 30 other Russian dissidents from Switzerland back to their homeland in a sealed railcar via Germany, Sweden, and Finland. The entourage arrived in Petrograd in April, and Lenin began assessing the situation and consolidating the Bolsheviks' position in the new Russia.[53]

By late fall, Lenin felt the time was right for him and his allies to make their move. On November 6, 1917, the Bolshevik Party executed a coup, forcibly taking control of the buildings that housed the Provisional Government, mostly former Romanov palaces, theaters, and public halls. The leaders were arrested. Bolshevik troops, with the Romanov palaces now in hand, vandalized the bourgeois art on the walls and helped themselves to the contents of the wine cellars.

The end of the Provisional Government was pronounced by the Party as the official birth of a new nation: the Russian Soviet Federative Socialist Republic, or RSFSR. As de facto head of state, Lenin, under increasing pressure from German attacks, signed a hastily-brokered Treaty of Brest-Litovsk, forfeiting much of Russia's empire in the Baltics and Eastern Europe in return for a cease-fire, international recognition, and consolidation. Russia finally had

---

53. A fascinating look at this negotiation, as well as the chaotic days of the Provisional Government, can be found in Merridale, *Lenin on the Train*.

peace, at least externally. Yet internally, things were far from settled. There was much to be done for Lenin and the Bolsheviks to truly take control.

BY JULY 1918, the royal family had been moved to a nondescript merchant's house in Yekaterinburg in the Ural Mountains. The home bristled with machine guns and armed guards. The family was rarely allowed outside and were constantly harassed and bullied by their captors, who dropped all pretension of royal deference.

One night, the family was awoken suddenly and told to dress for travel. They were hustled into the basement. The whole family was lined up along a wall and shot by Bolshevik revolutionaries. Their bodies were dissolved in acid and the remains thrown into a remote mineshaft, which was only rediscovered in 1979.

Despite rumors that young Anastasia escaped, in reality, none of the royal family survived. The Romanov line was cut off, and Russia as it had been for more than a thousand years effectively ceased to exist.

Soviet Russia emerged forged in blood and steel, rising out of chaos and disorder. But forging this new state, maintaining the momentum of revolution, and bringing about the utopia Lenin and the Bolsheviks promised would be a tall order.

9

CREATION: THE COMMUNIST EXPERIMENT

Lenin builds his communism | Wars and rumors of wars | Art, and the fight against it | Stalin rises | Fighting fascism

The first years of the Soviet Union were a heady time. It was an opportunity to experiment, to iterate, to work out Marxist philosophy and empower the long-suffering Russian people. The old empire was dead. The new leader, Lenin, had thousands of followers eager to overhaul Russian society from the top down. The Bolsheviks had near-unlimited power and resources to remake Russia into something new, something that severed all ties with the tsarist past, and chart a new course to improve the lot of the proletariat, powered by a zealous belief in Marxism.

The time to usher in an egalitarian utopia was here.

LENIN AND THE Bolsheviks got to work immediately. The capital of the RSFSR was moved from Petrograd, where the revolution had begun, to Moscow, which was both more centrally located and less tinted by capitalist and Romanov influences. Moscow thus became the nucleus of a new nation tied together not by blood or history but by ideology.

But what to do with the sprawling Romanov domain? Marxist thought rejected a repressive imperial-style government that forced minorities to submit to centralized power, so Lenin maneuvered: each region that might think of becoming independent got its own state, heading off the possibility of separatism. The Ukrainian Soviet Socialist Republic, Belarusian Soviet Socialist Republic, Kirghiz Soviet Socialist Republic, and others were formed, each governing its own area and people groups under socialist principles until communism's final victory could be brought about. Yet these were not truly independent nations; instead, all of them together, more than a dozen, made up the USSR,[54] the Union of Soviet Socialist Republics. Most all of them had to be conquered by the Bolshevik Red Army. There were no volunteer nations, eager to sign on to Lenin's socialist experiment.

And so, from 1918 to 1922, a bloody civil war raged.

---

54. The number hit 15 at the peak of the USSR in 1956, but the total varied throughout the state's history.

While the Bolsheviks, or "Reds," had a hold on power in the main metropolitan centers of Petrograd and Moscow, many saw the Revolution as a temporary extremist detour. Some, like the "Whites," even sought to reinstate a distant Romanov or held out hopes for liberal democracy. And there were other emboldened political and military factions at play, not to mention millions of frustrated troops who were still armed, deployed, and directionless.

Chaos reigned. In Russia's North, near Arkhangelsk, American troops landed in an effort to bolster White forces and prevent military stockpiles from falling into Bolshevik hands.[55] Along the Mongolian and Chinese border, former monarchist military officers set themselves up as local warlords and tried to create their own breakaway nations.[56] The Czechoslovak Legion, a force from Austrian imperial lands that had fought alongside tsarist Russia, was suddenly caught between hostile German armies and anti-tsarist Reds. With no direct route home, they were forced to navigate their way east across the breadth of Russia to Vladivostok, where Allied ships could take them back to Europe. After a long journey punctuated by daring military operations, more than 50,000 Czechoslovak soldiers made it home.[57]

In 1922, the last armed resistance to Lenin's Red Army was finally crushed and a union of nominally independent socialist states was proclaimed. But the Civil War had taken a brutal toll. From Poland to the Pacific, some 10 million people, men and women, civilian and military, were dead from battle, famine, and exposure. The new communist Russia had earned its legitimacy at the point of a bayonet. But the state was, at last, unified.

At the core of the new Soviet Union was the RSFSR, the largest, wealthiest, and most populous of all the republics. It was understood that the other republics would support the course set by Moscow and the political agenda set by the RSFSR. And the new direction proposed by the new Bolshevik government was a significant shift.

From the beginning, Lenin declared that the USSR was to be democratic; all citizens could vote and have a voice in government, unlike in Nicholas II's exclusive, puppet State Duma.[58] Reflecting this, the new class of bureaucrats, even high-ranking ones, were not the educated gentlemen of tsarist times, but rather working-class commoners who ended up in their positions with a little luck and good timing after making a name for themselves in the revolution, the Civil War, and the ensuing repressions. They were strike leaders, community organizers, and pamphlet writers who now became agency directors, department heads, and political candidates. While there was eventually only one political party (the Communist Party), citizens could choose between pre-screened candidates for government and leadership

---

55. Nelson, *The Polar Bear Expedition*, is the comprehensive history of this ill-fated campaign, which was the only time the American military has operated on Russian soil.

56. See Sunderland, *The Baron's Cloak*.

57. Edwards, "See Siberia by Train, Virtually."

58. Initially, the Bolsheviks intended to keep and strengthen the Duma. Nationwide elections were held in November 1917. Sixty-three million Russians voted, but when only about a quarter of them voted for the Bolshevik party, Lenin ordered the Duma dissolved. See Billington, *The Icon and the Axe*, 452

offices. Behind the scenes, votes rarely counted: Party members often simply appointed allies to official positions.

Indeed, the Communist Party itself, despite its democratic overtures, was in reality an exclusive club. Not only was it a political party; affiliation with the Party could open doors that might otherwise be firmly locked. Being a member carried huge social clout. Not everyone was guaranteed to make it in, but those who did could expect better housing, the ability to travel abroad with greater freedom, better educational opportunities, and much more besides. Leading the Party was the Politburo, the ruling council occupied by the most influential Party members. Members of the Politburo were the true power-holders of the Soviet state.

Anything (to say nothing of anyone) having ties with the old Romanov order was to be abandoned, destroyed, or repurposed to serve the needs of the people. Palaces, gardens, and art that had once been only accessible to the most privileged of society now belonged to the masses and became public museums and parks. Some precious works of art were sold to raise critical funds in those early days, and those that remained moved into public museums for the people's enjoyment. The Winter Palace is one example: after being taken by the Bolsheviks, it became a massive complex where visitors could not only tour the opulent rooms in which the Romanovs once lived but also enjoy works of fine art from around the globe. It retains this role today.

Religion, according to communist theory, had to be removed entirely, as it was, per Marx, a tool of the ruling class to placate and delude the worker – an "opiate of the masses." Countless churches and monasteries were torn down. Others, those that were iconic landmarks, were given new utility. One cathedral in St. Petersburg was converted into an ice skating rink; another became a museum of atheism and torture. Moscow's monumental Cathedral of Christ the Savior, built after victory over Napoleon, was bulldozed in the 1920s to make way for the Palace of the Soviets, a massive legislative complex to mark the victory of the proletariat. When construction stalled, leaving nothing but a large hole in the ground, authorities filled it with water and turned it into the world's largest outdoor swimming pool.[59] The church as an institution was stripped of almost all its power; local churches remained, but they moved squarely out of the public sphere as they were deemed an antiquated curiosity, an emblem of an unenlightened time, poison for the rationalistic communist mind and soul. Instead of Christmas as the major late-December holiday, Russians began to celebrate a secular New Year with fireworks, decorated indoor trees, social gatherings, and a speech from the Kremlin broadcast nationwide.

The Russian economy, for years hampered by shortages and technological lag, also had to be completely overhauled to bring about socialist prosperity. Following the end of the Civil War, Lenin implemented the New Economic Policy, or NEP, which moved away from "war communism," pulling back from outright collectivism and implementing Moscow-steered,

---

59. After all, recreation available to all was a communist value.

bourgeoisie-free state capitalism that would empower the worker to jumpstart production after years of devastation. But Lenin's retreat from a hard-line approach was fleeting: not long after he died, the Russian economy shifted back towards Marxist fundamentals, the basics of which characterized the USSR until its collapse. All major industries and commercial activities were placed in the hands of the state and thereby the people. International trade ceased, and all domestic production was refocused for self-sufficiency. Farms, once held by either village councils or in private hands, were turned into kolkhozes, collective farms owned by the entire village. Factories were turned over to the economic bureaus serving the central government in Moscow. Supply, demand, and prices were determined by planners in bureau offices.

But here the cracks in the Soviet system began to show. Even expert economists could misjudge a year's supply and demand, which could distort the entire economic system. If the prices set by the regime's experts were too low, stores could run out of items; too high, and items collected dust. And without competition or economic flexibility, the quality and quantity of goods were inconsistent. The iconic Soviet breadlines were caused by just this problem. Those who lived through the Soviet period often tell stories of entering a line outside a store merely because it was there. If others thought the line had something worth waiting for, it might be worth it to get in line, too.

And the problems went deeper. A shaky economy coupled with centralized power led to a system of widespread corruption and intrinsic distrust. With no consequences of doing a poor job and salaries flattened to promote the fundamental Marxist value of equality, getting high-quality goods, let alone finding someone trustworthy to do a job, could be difficult. Elected representatives and government bureaucrats instead operated on a system of personal patronage and Party favors. For common people, passing along a gift, monetary or otherwise, to a doctor could ensure closer attention; sending a bureaucrat a little cigarette money could mean that your application to change jobs, get a new house, or travel might be processed more quickly. Hence the quip that in the Soviet Union, you did not pay taxes; you just bribed the taxman to leave you alone.

Perhaps the best example of the Soviet system was the way in which it provided housing. Russian communism promised several social programs, many of which are progressive even today. All citizens were entitled to free medical care, education, and a state-funded pension, no matter their occupation, and women were especially encouraged to study and join the workforce. Yet housing, to which everyone was entitled, was a persistent problem. Quantity and equality took priority, which sidelined questions of durability, aesthetic beauty, and residents' quality of life. Early on in the USSR, a wave of peasants flocked to the cities, causing overcrowding. To solve this, many apartments were shared between multiple families. In a *kommunalka*, rooms might be further divided by hanging blankets or partitions, and the bathroom and kitchen were shared by all residents. As many as a half-dozen families might live in a city apartment once owned by a single middle-class family. In the 1950s, Soviet leader Nikita Khrushchev tried to solve this problem with prefabricated concrete buildings that turned out to be shoddy and prone to leaking or collapse. These edifices were designed with only five floors because architectural regulations stated that any building of more than five floors required an elevator and as such would be far more expensive to build. Instead of *kommunalkas*, many children of the later USSR grew up in these squat, sprawling *khrushchevkas*. Even today, Russians are almost all apartment-dwellers, with few owning and living in detached houses.

There were other sinister sides to the USSR, too. Those unwilling to join the new communist system found themselves arrested, in prison, or executed for working against the interests of the Party and liberated proletariat. To accomplish this, Alexander III's Okhrana found a successor in Lenin's secret police force, the Cheka. In the early years of the USSR, many prisoners were simply those with property who refused to turn it over to the new state in the initial nationalizing wave: businessmen, no matter their wealth, or kulaks, peasants that had become middle-class themselves (by, say, owning a single cow or small flock of sheep) since the freeing of the serfs and who were now reluctant to give their wealth up. As bourgeois capitalists and vestiges of the oppressive tsarist regime, they would have to be removed from the new Soviet utopia, along with anyone not willing to play by the new communist rules.

Who knows how much of this new society Lenin envisioned in November 1917. Regardless, it was his ambition, and the ambition of his circle, that remade Russia completely.

WITH THE NEW Bolshevik state finally established, the mood in civil society was youthfully optimistic, excited to see what the new USSR could achieve. A novelty itself, the new regime welcomed experimentation in almost any field, so long as they stuck to the Marxist ideology and forsook bourgeois themes. Vibrant new artistic movements, most notably in painting and film, began to form. Visual artists embraced avant-garde constructivism, which emphasized repetitive colors and abstract patterns. Early constructivist art echoed clanging heavy industry, a Soviet ideal that glorified the collectivized proletariat as a mere cog in a machine, minimized the importance of the individual, and celebrated the modern industrial state. Blocky geometric forms and repeating shapes and colors nodded towards the innovations that would provide a high standard of living to all workers now that Marx's theories were being brought to reality.[60]

Further, Lenin personally and fervently supported film as an innovative way to efficiently teach Soviet values to a large and diverse population, especially those with little formal education or literacy. Traveling car-borne projectors could roll into the most provincial town, set up in a disused church or village hall, and quickly imbue the residents with a working, if crude, knowledge of communist philosophy through visual storytelling.

Sergei Eisenstein was perhaps the most prolific Russian filmmaker and one of the most famous and well-regarded directors in history. Thanks to Lenin's patronage of the new medium of film, Eisenstein was given the leeway to use groundbreaking techniques to reinforce the communist message. His films, such as *Battleship Potemkin* (about the 1905

---

60. See D'Andrea and West, eds., *The Avante-Garde in Russia 1910-1930*.

In a shot from Eisenstein's Battleship Potemkin, *oppressive tsarist troops march down the steps of Odessa to quash the uprising. The repetition of boots here mirrors the constructivist artistic movement, abstracting the individual and instead focusing on the action of the masses. A still from Mosfilm.*

mutiny of the Russian navy ship) and *October: Ten Days That Shook the World* (retelling the November 1917 Revolution), told epic, Soviet-friendly sagas about the masses resisting unjust oppression, finding their voice and power to resist and fight back. He quickly became famous for his knack for glorifying everyday heroes who demonstrated themes of personal sacrifice for the good of the collective. Eisenstein, like other artists of the time, leveraged his talents for the goals of the communist revolution.[61]

LENIN WAS, TO the end, a true believer in the communist ideology, a born activist and revolutionary. Energetic, intellectual, charismatic, and passionate, he possessed a single-minded drive to see communism realized in Russia. Several tales grew up around him to demonstrate his dedication to the liberation of the Russian people: how he miraculously survived assassins' bullets, how he lived disguised as a Finnish farmer in a haystack, or how he began the Saturday civic cleanup subbotnik movement personally by spending a day

---

61. Beumers, *History of Russian Cinema*, is a comprehensive resource on Soviet film.

clearing debris from a post-Revolution Moscow street.[62] Lenin grew to be larger-than-life, an unimpeachable myth, someone who, in the popular imagination, forsook personal gain for the sake of the revolution.

On his death in 1924, just seven years after his installation as chairman of the Soviet Union, the Politburo decided to embalm their leader. For this purpose, a special building was constructed on Red Square just outside Moscow's Kremlin. Intended to be temporary, initially the mausoleum was made of wood. However, so many citizens came to pay their respects that the building was reconstructed in red and black marble in the clean, proletarian lines of constructivism. Petrograd's name was changed yet again, to Leningrad. Soon, almost every Russian town sported a bust, if not a full statue, of Lenin in its main square.

Who, now, could fill Lenin's shoes? To follow on one of the most critical personages in recent history was a tall order. Now that the foundation of the Soviet Union was laid, the next leader's work was clear: to continue Lenin's work by encouraging the spread of socialism to susceptible nearby states while maintaining momentum towards final communist revolution. Already in the early 1920s, three neighboring republics had been forced into a more socialist union: Ukraine, Belarus, and the Transcaucasus. But this was only the beginning of a USSR that was just starting to find its footing.

In 1927, after three years of political maneuvering, Joseph Stalin took the helm. His political instincts had led him to seize the post of the Party's General Secretary, putting him in charge of appointments. He used his position and personal shrewdness to outmaneuver, exile, unseat, and even kill any opponent. Notoriously, Stalin's most serious political rival was Leon Trotsky, leader of the Petrograd Soviet during the early days of the Revolution and a close associate of Lenin. With Stalin's rise, Trotsky was demonized and exiled from Russia. He took up residence in Mexico, but was eventually tracked down and assassinated with an ice pick by Soviet agents.

Stalin was not Russian by birth. He was born Ioseph Vissarionovich Dzhugashvili and raised in the hinterlands of the Russian Empire in Georgia, in the Caucasus Mountains. As a young man, he left Orthodox clerical training to pursue communist agitation under the pseudonym Koba, gaining some renown as a Robin Hood-esque bank robber. In the early twentieth century, he joined Lenin's Bolsheviks and commanded Red forces in the Civil War, proving himself a cunning and brave leader. By 1922, he had secured both a glowing reputation and a high position in the new Soviet government. He worked intimately with Lenin as part of his inner circle, the most powerful group in the USSR.[63]

Stalin may have, like Lenin, been a true believer in communism. But whereas Lenin promoted an image of himself as a fatherly leader, unafraid to work alongside the common

---

62. See Kononov, *Stories about Lenin*, for this and more delightful, yet dubious, propaganda. In one story, Lenin even takes on the role of Santa Claus, visiting an orphanage on a stormy New Year's Eve to play games with the children and distribute gifts.

63. See Khlevniuk, *Stalin*, for an authoritative look at the ruler's life.

Buddies: An older Lenin and younger Stalin, circa 1923. This is the famous image, discussed below, that Stalin ordered edited to make himself appear larger and stronger compared to an aging Lenin. In true communist fashion, this image is in the public domain.

laborer in unassuming clothing, sharing an encouraging comment and bearing a determined smile, Stalin held power far more dearly. He quickly gained a reputation for brutality fueled by paranoia and personal ego that made him the model of repressive authoritarianism for future generations. It is, perhaps, all in his name. Whereas Lenin took on a pseudonym that referred to a remote river in Russia's backcountry, embracing folk life and uplifting idyllic provincialism, the name "Stalin" has its root in the Russian word for steel: unbending, cold, and deadly, but the building block of the modern era.

The tone of Stalin's rule differed markedly from that of Lenin's. The second Soviet leader was willing to go to any length to sweep aside opposition and bring about the communist revolution. He built an apparatus that used terror and fear, envy and vindictiveness, to create a society-wide sense of dread and anxiety. The threat of being accused of making a careless remark, or merely being less than laudatory of the regime, leading to midnight arrest never to see one's family again, discouraged dissent. The imposing edifice of the secret police on Moscow's Lubyanka Square became infamous – a symbol of state surveillance, unjustified detainment, and merciless interrogation. While Lenin's secret police force, the Cheka, had ruthlessly rooted out bourgeois elements and foreign spies, Stalin's NKVD ramped up terror both within the Party and outside it, rooting out political rivals and invented enemies. Thousands could disappear over just a few days. Those suspected of anti-Soviet behavior, regardless of their innocence, could expect arrest, then questioning, a period of detention, and then a show trial in front of Party officials.

If they were not executed for their crimes, prisoners might be sent to the gulags, a system of over 400 work camps throughout the Soviet Union. The word "gulag" is an acronym-portmanteau from the Russian "Main Administration of Camps," referring to the bureaucratic office that handled their operation, but the word came to apply to the camps themselves.

The gulags built on the experience of the world's first concentration camps for political prisoners, which Lenin had implemented as a part of his socialist statebuilding in the 1920s. Gulags existed not so much to kill criminals but rather to extract their labor over a period of years and use it in aid of Stalin's massive public industrialization projects. It was gulag prisoners, by and large, who built the dams, canals, railroads, power generators, mines, and settlements that pushed Russia's economy forward and modernized its infrastructure. Often, gulags operated in remote and desolate regions, such as the Far North, Siberia, or the Pacific Coast, places where workers were unlikely to go voluntarily. Escape was nearly impossible; even if the fence was breached or the work gang was slipped away from, it could take weeks of travel to get anywhere settled. Inmates were provided minimal food and shelter by the prison system, but little else. They had just less than the bare necessities to keep them alive and working, all under the keen eye of guards. One inmate, Aleksandr Solzhenitsyn, survived the camps and would one day become an internationally renowned author, penning the semiautobriographical One Day in the Life of Ivan Denisovich, relating the day-to-day life of a prisoner, and the nonfiction Gulag Archipelago, an exposé of Stalin's brutality, as well as many other works. His writing put a human face to the inhuman scale of Stalin's repressions, although his works were only published after the leader's death. In 1970, Solzhenitsyn won the Nobel Prize for Literature in honor of his work.

It is hard to know how many people went through the gulag system, as records were routinely scrubbed and the worst state offenses covered up. Estimates reach 25 million labor camp prisoners under Stalin. During a peak period, 1936-37's Great Purge, Stalin engineered the death, imprisonment, and exile of an estimated 700,000 persons who he considered threats, ranging from security staff to high-ranking Party members to everyday workers. The death toll from Stalin's gulags might have topped 2.7 million, whether from overwork, medical problems, malnutrition, exposure, or other causes.

And yet gulags were just one cruel aspect of Stalin's regime. There were also the famines caused by both poor economic oversight and personal malice. Between 1930 and 1933, as Stalin's agricultural reforms led to inefficiencies and waste, agricultural production stuttered. A largely man-made famine raged throughout what was once one of Europe's most productive agricultural regions. Completely preventable, it was only worsened by government policies, in particular, Moscow's orders that other Soviet republics divert precious food to Russian citizens. As a result, four million died in Ukraine in what that country calls the Holodomor, and more than a million more died in other Soviet republics.

All told, by the end of Stalin's time in office, an estimated 20 million Soviets had perished as a result of his policies, be it from execution, starvation, overwork, forced industrialization, or other causes. This figure places Stalin among the most brutal dictators in history.

Stalin's sins might have undermined his rule, but his iron fist also squeezed the media. In Stalin's Russia, the truth itself was malleable. It was just another tool to ensure compliance.

The regime's worst offenses were simply covered up. At the height of the 1930-33 famine, for instance, train cars traveling through affected regions had their windows covered, and the international press was presented a much rosier picture than the reality. Some in the West even applauded Stalin's progressive agricultural initiatives while millions starved.

Further, Stalin's regime churned out waves of propaganda in all media, censoring anything even remotely critical or dangerous to the regime. Shortly after his rise to power, he had a well-known photograph of himself and Lenin manipulated so that he appeared larger and more prominent. And throughout his career, he ordered images touched up to add drama, remove blemishes, and even extract those that had fallen out of favor.

The duration and depth of Stalin's policies cultivated a new, specifically Soviet culture that expanded on and twisted what the first exuberant generation of communist artists under Lenin had produced. Under Stalin, experimentation in art and film were reigned in and redirected into a movement called socialist realism. Gone were the days of impersonal abstraction or refined beauty, which smacked of capitalistic decadence and ivory-tower scholasticism. Paintings and statues now took the form of realistic, if idealized, scenes from the lives of workers. Themes might include bulky women cheerily harvesting grain in the sun, a half-naked man pulling a lever in a large, powerful factory, or children quietly studying to build communism for the next generation. The tones are serious, literal, and workaday, elevating labor with little subtlety. This was art for the people, reminding workers in simple visual terms of their duty to the ongoing revolution as they went about their everyday lives. This new artistic language also led to a specifically Stalinist architecture style, coupling awe-inspiring gigantism and hard-edged utilitarianism that demonstrated the power of the state and uplifted the proletariat in the spaces he inhabited every day. Elaborate lifelike statues adorned public transit stops, colorful mosaics punctuated concert hall lobbies, and gymnasiums featured murals impelling athletes to train for the sake of the communist revolution.

Likewise, in film, more straightforward stories of the ideal Soviet hero-man, who was simple, rational, and willing to sacrifice himself, became the norm. The archetype of this genre is 1934's *Chapaev*, a biopic of a Russian Civil War commander. He and his motley band of commoner-troops stubbornly fight off aristocratic Whites on the steppes of Russia. Vasily Chapaev himself is humorless and simple, a working man forced to fight who explains military strategy with potatoes, but a charismatic and confident leader with unwavering tenacity for the Bolshevik cause. In the film's final scene, Chapaev sacrifices himself so his men can achieve victory. Supposedly *Chapaev* was based on a true story, but here, as elsewhere under Stalin, the storytellers could play fast and loose with the truth to serve political ends.[64]

One of the most notable films of this time is Eisenstein's later work, *Alexander Nevsky*, released in 1938. It was under Stalin, and in Eisenstein's hands, that Nevsky's life gained new meaning for a more modern Russia. Perhaps no film is a better example of how the Soviet state imbued communist meaning into everything it created.

Alexander Nevsky took all the excitement and emotional evocations that Eisenstein was known for and applied it to the new Stalinist cultural mold, making *Alexander Nevsky* squarely a product of socialist realism. Eisenstein was reportedly supervised by Party stooges throughout filming and was considerably more constrained than during his previous projects like *Battleship Potemkin*. There is little ambiguity or experimentation; the plot is straightforward, simple, and literal. The Prince Alexander Nevsky shown in the film is portrayed as an idealized Soviet man, just like Chapaev. Nevsky has no romantic interest; the defense of Russia is his only goal. Further, the medieval Russia of the film is a glossy Marxist reinterpretation of 13th-century Novgorod: clean, industrious, and agnostic, ruled by the masses whose liberated labor is achieved with jaunty, dedicated gusto. The German invaders, however, are the opposite: inhuman, stratified, suspicious, brutish, and fanatically, superstitiously religious – the antithesis of Soviet values. German troops sport stormtrooper-style helmets, and some even wear swastikas. The film concludes with Nevsky imploring, "Those who come at us with the sword will be beaten back with the sword!" That final line soon adorned propaganda posters that depicted medieval Novgorodian horsemen charging Panzer tanks as the film soared in popularity in the 1940s.

Other media were not untouched, either. Even newspapers could publish complete lies in support of Stalin's authoritarian communist worldview. Perhaps most emblematic was the tale of Pavlik Morozov, published in newspapers as fact in 1933. According to the Soviet press, young Pavlik, a star student and leader of his school's Young Pioneers group, caught his father engaging in capitalistic activities and reported him to authorities. His father was duly arrested and executed for undermining the revolution. Yet Pavlik's family were angered that he believed so fully in Soviet justice. And so they killed him, dumping his body in a meadow. Local police and Party leadership, after learning what had happened, rounded up the family and had them,

---

64. Chapaev today lives on as the subject of many sarcastic jokes making fun of his too-serious folk logic.

A German priest in Eisenstein's Alexander Nevsky *wears a mitre adorned with Nazi symbols. A still from Mosfilm, public domain.*

in turn, killed by firing squad. The press hailed Pavlik as a model Soviet child, a glorious martyr for the continuing revolution, and his image graced books, statues, and more.

Of course, Pavlik's story was a fabrication, but it held a deeper truth about the Stalinist period – that the state could even infiltrate and dissolve the close ties of family. The news of the time was an unreliable narrator, but state-approved, and so must be believed. Thus did the constant surveillance, totalitarian policing, and government doublespeak of Stalin's Russia inspire some of the earliest dystopian novels, most directly George Orwell's *1984*.

Indeed, state repression under Stalin served a greater purpose: endorsing unquestioned state power so that the country could be forced down a path of sweeping modernization. By monopolizing the media, the state could cover up outrages and tell tales only of victory, omitting anything that might tarnish it. Thus, ill-informed outside observers and communist allies alike praised the construction of massive river canal projects, Moscow's and Leningrad's clockwork metro systems, and progressive social services, while the horrors of gulags and famines went unreported. With no meaningful impediments to his power, Stalin oversaw a radical shift in the Soviet economy, away from agriculture and towards heavy industry, machinery, and mechanization. By 1940, Russia was approaching economic output levels of Western states, and, in light of the Great Depression wracking the West, the Soviet system held a certain appeal (at least, for those who did not experience it for themselves).

The true test, however, of the state Stalin had built would come from outside. And for all the holes in the system, for all the repressions and terrors, the Soviet Russia Stalin had formed was formidable.

STALIN'S SOVIET UNION and Adolf Hitler's Nazi Germany had been on a collision course for almost a decade. On one hand, ideologically, communists and fascists viewed each other as irreconcilable enemies. On the other, geopolitically, Germany needed the grain, coal, steel, and oil of Central Europe and the Caucasus to fuel its growing military. Both states were further united in that they were pariahs in the 1920s and 1930s, outside the established European order; Russia helped Germany secretly rearm and retrain in violation of World War I treaty restrictions,[65] and German expertise and machinery contributed to Soviet industrialization.

In September 1939, the USSR and Nazi Germany signed the Molotov-Ribbentrop Pact. For both sides, this was a marriage of convenience between two wary competitors. It established an attitude of cautious nonaggression between the two authoritarian states and split much of Eastern Europe between them. Hitler was free to engage Poland and France without Soviet involvement, and Stalin felt secure enough of the unlikelihood of a European war that he conducted an untimely purge of the military's officer corps.

So when the German army suddenly turned and attacked Russia on the night of June 22, 1941, it caught Stalin unawares. Hitler, like Napoleon, believed that all that was needed was to take key cities and the nation would surrender. German weapons, tanks, and planes vastly outnumbered and outperformed their Russian counterparts, and many soldiers were already veterans of successful campaigns of conquest. By all accounts, Germany had the advantage in troops, equipment, and experience. Nazi tanks, planes, and troop transports blitzkrieged east as the Soviet Union was caught on the back foot.

Yet, just three weeks after the initial attack, it was apparent that Russia would not be a pushover. In less than a month, more German troops had died in the Soviet campaign than in all Nazi operations in Europe to that point combined.

The German military had severely underestimated Soviet capabilities. Stalin's initiatives for industrialization, plus massive reserves of manpower, helped stem the tide. Factories swiftly upped production to push out tanks and aircraft, manned by fervent citizens eager to drive the Germans from their soil. Even as many factories were moved further into the interior of the country, away from the front, combat experience allowed for refinement and improvement of war materiel. Further, Russian conscripts were fighting on their home turf for the very preservation of their nation, fueled by the ideological refinement Stalin had shaped over his years in the Kremlin. The Germans were in for stiff resistance.

But Russian forces still found themselves losing ground. By September 1941, Leningrad was under siege, surrounded by German troops, with civilians doggedly clinging to survival through constant shelling and air raids. Nazis were also at the gates of Moscow by that October. Many in the city were evacuated to Ural factory towns to keep up the war effort

---

65. For instance, German engineers working at the Kama Tank School outside Kazan designed the Panzer tank there in the 1920s, and pilots trained at an airfield in Lipetsk. Collaboration of this type declined sharply once the Nazi government came to power in 1933.

away from the fighting. Still, Leningrad and Moscow held out, and Russian troops doggedly delayed the invaders, giving the nation precious time and space to mobilize and dig in.

And then, as the year progressed, Hitler met the same force that had stopped Napoleon in his tracks: bad weather. Fall rains created *rasputitsa* quagmires in the roads, halting the German advance as tanks and trucks floundered. Soon, the invading army was stuck in unfriendly territory with unreliable supply lines, dug in with inadequate equipment for one of the coldest winters on record. Tanks and aircraft that gave the German army an edge over its opponents simply did not work in the Russian cold. And just like in previous wars, little improved come spring: snowmelt just created more mud and *rasputitsa*. And all the while, the winter reprieve allowed the Russians to regroup and fortify so as to better hold out against the invaders.

With Leningrad and Moscow pinned down, Hitler looked southward, to a small city on the Volga called Stalingrad. It was a major transit center between inland Russia, the Black Sea, and the Caucasus. In addition, its very name made it a symbol of Soviet power. If the Germans could take Stalingrad, it would not only be a blow to Russian morale; it would also open up a path to the oil fields in the south to keep fueling the advance.

The battle for Stalingrad lasted six months, from July 1942 to February 1943. After the initial offensive reached a stalemate, both sides continued to pour millions of troops into the city. The battle devolved into house-by-house fighting over shells of ruined buildings. But the Soviets were victorious, encircling and capturing much of what remained of the German 6th Army, defending the city through brutal and nightmarish close-quarters combat. By the end, as many as three million soldiers were dead on Stalingrad's rubble-strewn streets. The Battle of Stalingrad became the single bloodiest engagement in human history. A Russian counterattack at Kursk in July and August 1943 drove Axis forces from the Volga region and decisively turned the tide in southern Russia and in the war.

By this time, up north, the siege of Leningrad had dragged on for over two years, becoming a more-than-desperate situation. Scarce food led city officials to infuse ration bread with sawdust. After public utilities were destroyed, water was collected from holes in the street left from German artillery shells.[66] There were rumors of cannibalism. The Hermitage collection was removed from the city for its own safety; legend has it that docents provided tours to soldiers on leave, describing each work verbally at its empty frame. And the same cold that killed Germans in their trenches served as a lifeline for the Russian civilians in Leningrad – subarctic winter froze local lakes and rivers, which meant that some inhabitants could be evacuated and more supplies could arrive from friendly lines over the ice. The siege, which had begun in the fall of 1941, was only lifted in January 1944, at the cost of millions of civilian and soldier lives.

---

66. Even today, sharp-eyed tourists can spy notices on building walls advising which side of the road is safest from arcing artillery fire.

Yevgeny Khaldei's famous photograph of the capture of Berlin, with Stalinist artistic license added.

By 1944, Nazi Germany, now under Allied attack from the south and west and sustained aerial bombardment in its homeland, began to implode. The USSR gained momentum through its battlefield victories, slowly pushing German formations further and further west, on a quick march to Berlin, intent on capturing Germany's capital before its ally-rivals could.

In May 1945, the Red Army entered the city. Propaganda photographers staged, edited, and distributed what is now an instantly recognizable photograph of a soldier waving the Soviet flag over the ruins of the German Reichstag.

Hitler died by his own hand. Germany fell. The war was over. The USSR was victorious.

An estimated 30 million Soviets, 15 percent of the total pre-war population, had been casualties in the worst conflict the world had ever seen. The Soviet Union now controlled half of Europe, occupying many lands formerly under German control. But these new borders brought it face-to-face with the other great power that had emerged from the war: the United States.

In the past, the U.S. could have ignored a Soviet threat. But now, the USSR had growing influence, elevated international standing, and a determined, confident, battle-hardened citizenry. Stalin had cooperated with Franklin Roosevelt and Winston Churchill to conduct the war as allies, but the relationship had always been strained. Now, with no common enemy tying them together, Russia was emboldened. So was the West.

The Soviet Union that Lenin had founded, Stalin had solidified, and the war had refined faced a brave new world. By many measures, the new Soviet state was flourishing. It had stood a grueling test. The future was bright.

IN 2016, A new theme park opened in Moscow's western suburbs: Patriot Park. The nearly 14,000-acre complex could best be described as a military-themed Disneyland. Massive exhibit halls house tanks, fighter jets lounge on tarmac, and visitors can try out military training in indoor obstacle courses and shooting galleries.

But the core of the park hearkens to the dark years of 1941-45. A recreated "partisan village" lets tourists experience what it was like to be a guerilla sabotaging the German advance. Up to five thousand reenactors can relive the Battle of Berlin in front of a replica Reichstag, complete with landing strip so Messerschmitts can fly overhead.

The centerpiece of the park, the Main Cathedral of the Russian Armed Forces, sports a cupola exactly 19.45 meters in diameter. Below it is a saintly mosaic of Alexander Nevsky, flanked by Vladimir the Great and Boris and Gleb, appearing in the heavens above a mass of 1940s-era soldiers. And above it all float the closing words of Eisenstein's 1938 film: "Those who come at us with the sword will be beaten back with the sword."

If there is a single historical event that influences modern-day Russia more than any other, it is the Second World War. It would be difficult to overstate the role that World War II plays in the Russian conception of self. It is the single most significant point in history of the past century, but even saying that is an understatement when discussing how Russian society views it.

In Russia, the term "Great Patriotic War" is used far more often than "Second World War."[67] When Russians think of the conflict, they think of the sacrifices from their own families for the heroic defense of their nation. Russian casualties, both military and civilian, were by some estimates sixty times higher than those America suffered. Everyone knows of a family member who served, and almost everyone knows of a family member who died. There is simply no historical analog in the West.

As a result, Russia's main patriotic holiday is Victory Day, which marks the end of the war in Europe. It is celebrated each May 9 with military parades, speeches, and demonstrations. Russians memorialize the war obsessively, with everything from traveling train-car museums[68] to meticulous reenactments.[69] Countless movies, books, video games, and TV shows highlight Russia's role and sacrificial heroism. Towering monuments with mounted tanks, artillery, and planes or eternal flame monuments are ubiquitous markers in both Russian cities and small towns. These memorials are local landmarks, sites of community life, where children

---

67. Here, the word "patriotic," *otechestvennaya*, could also mean "fatherland."

68. Edwards, "Victory Train: Coming Soon to a Hero-City Near You."

69. Edwards, "The Motherland Calls... Reenactors."

lay wreaths and young couples take wedding photos. They are integrated into the everyday business of the city and venerated with religious devotion. It would not be a stretch to call the war sacred, the Holy of Holies of Russian history, a myth that is completely untouchable by modern scrutiny, let alone criticism. Hence the 2021 law making it illegal to insult a veteran of the war.[70]

And as the modern Russian state tells it, the Great Patriotic War teaches that Russia must not trust anyone in the West. According to the Russian narrative, while the blood of millions of Soviets was spilled, Britain and the U.S. were far away, unwilling to help in any meaningful way and happy to let the Germans kill as many Russians as they wanted. The sheer scale of Russian bloodletting shows plainly that it was Russia, and no one else, who truly defeated Hitler and the fascists. Every Russian, therefore, should seek to sacrifice themselves in the same way, goes the narrative, and those who disagree are no better than traitors.

ON MAY 9, 2025, Russia celebrated eighty years since the end of the Great Patriotic War with one of the largest Victory Day parades in decades. Troops from around the world marched through Red Square beneath the famous photo of the Soviet hammer and sickle flying over Berlin. Some troops wore Second-World-War era gear and carried the flags of especially heroic regiments. After them came a handful of iconic T-34 tanks. New that year were trucks used for launching drones used in Ukraine.[71]

The Kremlin works hard to remind its citizens of the importance of that victory as wars on other fronts continue.

---

70. AFP, "Russia Bans Insults Against WWII Veterans."

71. Edwards, "One for the Books."

10

STAGNATION: THE COLD WAR
AND THE END OF THE COMMUNIST DREAM

The new world order | The fall of Stalin | The USSR lurches | Soviet life
| To the cosmos | And back to dust

When American author John Steinbeck visited the Soviet Union in 1947, he saw a nation that was beaten, yet optimistic; bloodied, but far from broken. Kiev was "a semi-ruin. Here the Germans showed us what they could do."[72] Moscow's Gorky Park housed a "war trophy display... And walking among the weapons were soldiers with their children and their wives, explaining these things professionally. The children looked with wonder at the equipment their fathers had helped to capture."[73] Citizens' abject existence in the smoldering remains of war-torn Stalingrad were "a strange and heroic travesty on modern living."[74] Everywhere he went, it seemed, the shadow of the invasion lingered.

Yet he also wandered to places where it almost seemed as if the war had not occurred at all. In Kiev, Steinbeck watched children swimming in the Dnieper as bands played in covered pergolas and couples strolled on a summer afternoon. In Georgia, he watched traditional wrestling. And in Moscow, in between formal dinners with Soviet writer's organizations, he attended parades, aerobatic displays, and fireworks celebrating the city's 800th birthday.

The Soviet Union Steinbeck was permitted to see (likely only due to his earlier pro-labor work, *The Grapes of Wrath*) sent a message: that the USSR was a vibrant alternative to the oppressive system of the capitalist West, that it was successful in fulfilling the promises of Marx to grant the good life to the lowliest Russian. But was it tenable in the long term? Could the promises of material comfort and state glory be maintained into the future?

THE USSR EMERGED from the Great Patriotic War as a great power. Communism had been vindicated on the battlefield. And now, with peace secured, the USSR could move into communist uptopia and set about spreading the workers' revolution around the globe.

---

72. Steinbeck, *Russian Journal*, 51.

73. Ibid, 109.

74. Ibid, 115.

After the war's end, out of the lands seized from the Germans, Stalin carved new Soviet states with their own communist governments: Poland, the Czech Republic, East Germany, Bulgaria, Romania, Yugoslavia, and Hungary. These were added to the Baltic nations already press-ganged into the Soviet Union through the 1939 pact: Latvia, Lithuania, and Estonia. The German city of Berlin was split between Moscow's control and administration by the West. These new territories came to be known as the Eastern Bloc. They were European communist countries, de facto subject states to Russia.

Russia's status as one of the world's geopolitical poles was cemented with its permanent appointment to the UN's Security Council when it was founded in 1945. Paradoxically, it had become a fearsome representative of a way of thinking that was antagonistic to existing international institutions, yet its socialist ideology and wartime success also made it appealing to many in the post-war era, as empires collapsed and nationalism swelled.

In 1949, American analysts noticed a strange radio signal emanating from a remote part of Siberia that matched an atomic test, so they asked the Soviets if it had been. Officials flatly denied it. Then, the next day, the Kremlin announced with great pomp that they had successfully tested a nuclear weapon. The nuclear age had begun.

The U.S., having already created and used a bomb that could obliterate entire cities, now faced the prospect of a USSR that could turn those same weapons on Western population centers. Given this reality, a conventional war between the U.S. and USSR seemed unthinkable. A Cold War ensued; East and West competed ideologically, militarily, and economically, while each accumulated massive nuclear arsenals that could never be used.

On March 3, 1953, Joseph Stalin died at the age of 74. The dictator had suffered only a minor stroke, but fear of reprisal paralyzed his inner circle into inaction, and many of the most experienced doctors in the Soviet Union had been imprisoned or killed. Gogol-esque bungling in the critical hours after the stroke sealed Stalin's fate. He was interred in the Red Square mausoleum alongside Lenin, and the granite inscription was changed to bear both their names.

Seventy years after his death, Stalin's legacy is complex. His image towers over the rest of Russian history. He is a figure of nuance, his contributions the center of debate. There is no neat solution to how Russians ought to remember him.

Since the end of the Soviet Union, typically, older Russians have viewed Stalin more favorably than those from the younger generations. Those that grew up in the USSR of the 1940s and 1950s were fed on a myth of Stalin's accomplishments and celebrated his victory in the Great Patriotic War. His human rights abuses, like the gulags and famines, were eventually acknowledged as terrible, but necessary for Stalin to achieve his ends and lead Russia into its position of prominence. By contrast, younger generations, who were exposed to a more full picture of Stalin tempered by Western media and values, saw him as neutral or even evil. A minority of those under age 30 saw him favorably.

Until recently. In 2019, for the first time in 20 years, a majority of Russians (51 percent) viewed Stalin favorably.[75] This indicated a shift in how young people think of him, likely informed by changes in Russia's retelling of its own past that again glorify Stalin and the USSR he built. And, indeed, a rehabilitation for Stalin has been ongoing. In May 2025, a new statue of him was unveiled at Taganskaya Station in the Moscow Metro, a recreation of a monument that was dismantled during station renovations in the 1960s.[76] It is merely one of several Stalin monuments appearing and re-appearing throughout Russia in the 2020s.

AS HAD HAPPENED after the death of Lenin, Stalin's death ushered in a period of political jockeying. It was eventually Nikita Khrushchev who took over the position of General Secretary. While Khrushchev had been loyal to Stalin as a member of the Politburo, and indeed took part in his repressions, he also sought to distance himself. Three years after Stalin's death, Khrushchev gave a "Secret Speech" to Soviet delegates at a closed conference explicitly denouncing Stalin and his methods of rule. The shocking address quickly leaked. It not only acknowledged the scale of the repressions and gruesome punishments that Stalin implemented but promised a turn away from them. No longer would the leader of the Soviet Union be put on a pedestal, revered as near-divine, with busts in every town square and photographs in every classroom. Khrushchev set about creating a more friendly-faced Soviet dictatorship, spearheading an era of "de-Stalinization." To kick it off, the late leader was reinterred just behind Lenin's Mausoleum to a venerated spot along the Kremlin wall.

Khrushchev maintained the goal of moving the socialist Soviet state ever closer towards true communism; in fact, he predicted its arrival within 20 years. He merely wanted to do so with a bit less terror and slave labor. If the USSR was to survive long-term, changes had to be made. Stalin's system, albeit ruthlessly effective in crisis and while pushing for modernization, was simply too harsh and unsustainable for flourishing in peacetime.

The use of gulags dramatically decreased, and many prisoners were allowed to return home. Censorship was loosened a bit, and freedom of art and expression were allowed some breathing room. Painters had more license for diverse and creative subjects. More avant-garde expression was still frowned upon as dangerous to the revolutionary cause and reveling in bourgeois frivolity, but films of the period often outright (if lightly) mocked the stodgy officiousness of the old-fashioned Stalinists. For example, 1956's *Carnival Night* cast a pompous theater director, sporting bushy brows and a Stalinesque suit, as a villain, constantly antagonized by easygoing, laughing youngsters just looking for a good time, often at his expense. Later, 1975's *The Irony of Fate* had a drunk man crash at an apartment he mistook for his own in St. Petersburg, not his native Moscow, a confusion caused by the same street name, same building, same apartment number, and same floorplan. The film was a humorous dig at the ubiquitous, gray, uninspired, mass-produced, monstrous architecture of Soviet

---

75. Levada Center, "Dynamika otnosheniya k Stalinu."

76. Rosenberg, "What a new Stalin statue says about Russia's attempt to reshape history."

towns, the planned complexes cheaply engineered to meet high housing demand. While in Stalin's time these films would have been near-treasonous, now, under Khrushchev, they were part of building a fresh Soviet worldview that was unafraid to self-deprecate and openly disavowed the insecurity of the past. Further, the Soviet economy became a bit more flexible. A pragmatist with a personal connection to Ukraine, Khrushchev overhauled the agricultural system Lenin and Stalin had built, loosened Stalin's strict controls over the markets, and encouraged limited international trade.

The new leader also pushed for a better and broader educational system, one that would make Soviet institutions a beacon of learning and research. Scientific advancement was prioritized, insofar as innovation meant prestige and legitimacy for the communist alternative. After all, Marx's communism promised not just a competitive system but the ideal system, one that could outstrip any capitalist society. And science not only reinforced socialist superiority; it could also give the USSR a military advantage.

It was against this backdrop that the Space Race was launched in 1957, when Sputnik was sent into orbit. A two-foot-diameter orb with four antennae trailing from it, Sputnik[77] was the first man-made object to successfully orbit the earth. Next, the Russians moved on to animals. The same year, a stray dog named Laika became the first animal to travel in space. However, scientists had failed to make plans for her return, and so she died on her mission. Two more strays, Belka and Strelka, along with a crew of mice, rabbits, and other animals and plants, next made a round trip after orbiting the earth 17 times. They returned as national heroes, and today, Belka and Strelka are stuffed and housed in a Moscow museum to be adored by fans for eternity.[78]

In 1961, the USSR switched to human cosmonauts, and Yuri Gagarin became the first man to orbit Earth. Two years later, Valentina Tereshkova, at age 26, became the first woman to reach space. Gagarin and Tereshkova were held up as symbols of Soviet ingenuity and perseverance, proof that the USSR had the resources, scientists, and dedication to achieve things no other country had before, not even the capitalist West. Gagarin died in a fighter jet crash only a few years after his flight, but Tereshkova later joined the Russian legislature, where she still serves at nearly 90.

These cosmic victories spoke to the strength of the Soviet way of life and legitimized the USSR as a competitor to the West. However, momentum eventually sputtered, and the USSR was unable to answer when the U.S. placed a man on the moon in 1969. And the still-secretive nature of Soviet society obfuscated what may have been a less successful program than what the public saw; after all, accidents and failures were certainly not publicized. For instance, when cosmonaut Valentin Bondarenko died in 1961 during an experiment at a Moscow research facility, his existence was completely covered up by the Soviet state. He was edited out

---

77. The name means "fellow traveler" or "satellite."

78. A family-favorite retelling of Belka and Strelka's story is Southgate, *Dogs in Space*.

From left to right, space travelers Yuri Garagin, Pavel Popovich, and Valentina Tereshkova share a laugh with earthling Nikita Khrushchev atop Lenin's Mausoleum in central Moscow in a 1963 photo from Soviet state media.

of photos and his death was not reported for nearly 20 years. It is possible, and not unlikely, that more cosmonauts perished than are recorded, along with decades of man-hours of labor and countless millions of rubles.

IN 1964, AN aging Khrushchev was deposed by the Politburo. His reforms had started strong, but his unpredictability and willful behavior was eventually confronted by the massive Soviet bureaucracy and entrenched political interests, who wanted greater stability. This they got in Leonid Brezhnev, who turned away from Khrushchev's liberal de-Stalinizing policies, ushering in more security, but also a new wave of censorship to art, music, and literature. An era of stagnation was underway.

Cracks began to appear in the Soviet facade. Now in its fifth decade, the Soviet experiment came face-to-face with the limits of forced industrialization. While big factories and awe-inspiring infrastructure projects had served to ramp up production capacity, an economy in which every input and output was tightly controlled by planning bureaucrats could never be sufficiently innovative and nimble to keep up with the challenges at play in the post-war world. In the absence of markets and true economic incentives for workers or businesses, output lagged and quality declined. The economy, and society as a whole, became plagued with corruption and self-dealing.

Soviet line for scarce underwear, 1981 (Irkutsk; credit Chtoe)..

Brezhnev and his cabinet blustered on the world stage, but they were living off stolen prestige won by Stalin and Khrushchev. Socialism was beginning to lose face. The Soviet world was beginning to crumble. The waning of Stalinist terror, combined with faltering socialist economies, led to popular rebellions in Eastern Bloc satellite states. When the uprisings had to be put down by tanks and occupation, it revealed for all the lie that undergirded the communist experiment. As Western free markets boomed, Soviet and East European states experienced regular shortages, shoddy goods, and snaking breadlines. And none of this could be effectively hidden from the prying eyes of visitors and Western news media, despite strict controls over the borders and media.

The information flow worked both ways. Unlike in Peter the Great's time, when the state had led a concerted effort to import new ideas, modern technology and globalization made it difficult to stem the trickle of cultural artifacts that were entering Russia organically. Music, fashion, and literature seeped in despite state controls. Younger generations who saw visiting outsiders wearing blue jeans and listening to pop music began to yearn for something different. Soviet authorities, meanwhile, jammed radio broadcasts of BBC, Radio Free Europe, and other Western stations to prevent their citizens from listening in, but those determined to hear found ways around the restrictions. Dedicated fans of banned foreign rock sometimes even repurposed discarded medical x-rays into black, plastic records which still bore images of bones. Many who had a chance to travel outside the country, like athletes and musicians, expressed wonder at life outside the USSR. Sometimes they simply chose not to return, wandering off when supervision was light.

Moscow was struggling to keep up as the global economy in the developed world shifted from heavy industry to high-tech, electronic, and computer manufacturing. While the former had been the bedrock on which Lenin and Stalin had built Soviet labor, the latter required robust educational infrastructure and an open, entrepreneurial culture. As a consequence, Soviet military technology became increasingly outdated and uncompetitive compared to Western weaponry and vehicles. Should the Cold War come to blows, it was becoming increasingly unlikely that the Soviet Union would be able to hold its own against its enemies. Further, many Russians still lived in cramped, crumbling, leaky apartments, built to past Soviet standards, or even below if bribes had been paid. These paled in comparison to homes elsewhere, kitted out with the newest appliances, which were simply unaffordable to the everyday Russian.

Events like the botched Soviet invasion of Afghanistan, where thousands of Soviet troops died needlessly, and growing anticommunist sentiment in communist Poland, Hungary, and East Germany only further undermined the Party's legitimacy. They underlined the need for change and fueled growing domestic disillusionment with the regime. The Soviet government, which was supposed to represent youthful, excited, communist progress, was beginning to look like an out-of-touch group of stolid old men who were xenophobic and scared of change. In a twist, the roles were reversed: the communists were looking a bit like the late Romanovs.

Brezhnev's initial successors, Yuri Andropov and Konstantin Chernenko, continued in his path. Their rules were short, yet they maintained strict control over the Soviet satellite states, discouraged dissent at home, and did little to fix the tailspinning economy. Atrophy and apathy had set in. In 1985, however, a new leader, Mikhail Gorbachev, entered Russia's story.

Gorbachev saw the failures of the Soviet Union and decided that the best way to rectify them was to bring some of the best of what the West had to offer to help invigorate Soviet society and its economy. If he could marry measured capitalist adaptability with centralized communist power, the USSR might survive, perhaps even thrive. The two buzzwords of Gorbachev's administration were perestroika and glasnost. Perestroika, Russian for "restructuring," focused on shifting the Soviet economy from a centralized command structure to a more local, responsive one that would be dynamic and in tune with supply and demand. Glasnost, meaning "openness," would lessen many of the restrictions on speech, media, and travel.

Gorbachev presented himself as an intelligent politician with deep convictions, but he was unpopular with some of his fellow leaders, who saw the changes as a betrayal of Lenin's proletarian revolution and a diversion from the goal of true communism, not to mention a threat to their own power. Soon, foreign businesses and fast-food chains opened in Russia, international tourists mobbed the Kremlin, and the Soviet people became increasingly exposed to a way of life that had been hidden from them for so long. All of this weakened Moscow's iron-fisted power, and the old guard of politicians raised from birth to serve authoritarian communism were not happy.

The system Gorbachev inherited was deeply flawed, and without the staunch support of communist elites backed by loyal Red Army soldiers, the Soviet-imposed regimes of many of the USSR's satellite states soon found themselves facing angry mobs of citizens calling for full-

A 1990 Russian state news photo of massive crowds gathering at the first McDonald's restaurant in Russia, Moscow, thanks to Gorbachev's political and economic reforms.

fledged liberal democracy. These demonstrations revealed just how lethargic the system had become and how impatient for change citizens were. In 1988, Poland took a democratic turn at the behest of blue-collar port workers, who organized for anticommunist causes through labor unions.[79] In East Germany, in 1989, an uninformed bureaucrat misspoke at a press conference, starting a chain of events that led to the dismantling of the Berlin Wall. Other states of the Eastern Bloc soon followed suit, turning to independence and often integration with the West. However, the republics directly in the USSR – Ukraine, Turkmenistan, Belarus, and others – remained firmly under Moscow's supervision.

Gorbachev's reforms were well intentioned, but they signaled the death knell of Marxist socialism in Russia. No longer would intolerable actions that endangered the Soviet way of life be prosecuted with arrest and gulag sentences, no longer would the USSR propagate isolation and suspicion. But how could the system go on, now that the dam had burst? How could the Soviet Union ever return to Lenin's or Stalin's vision now that it had compromised with half-measures and welcomed capitalists into the country? Gorbachev's reforms were impossible to roll back.[80]

---

79. Ironic.

80. A crucial resource on the last days of the USSR and the formative years of modern Russia is Ostrovsky, *The Invention of Russia*.

Amid the changes, Russian politics became more chaotic, and political restructuring caused uncertainty as to who truly held power. Still, there was public sentiment for a unified state: a USSR-wide referendum in March 1991 found that almost 80 percent of Soviet citizens wanted to maintain a reformed Soviet Union. Most of the Baltic and Caucasian republics boycotted the vote.

Then, in June of that year, the USSR held its first open presidential election. The former communist leader of Moscow, Boris Yeltsin, won the presidency of the RSFSR with 57 percent of the vote, overtaking the establishment's preferred candidate, while Gorbachev remained the head of the USSR. Yeltsin was a strong supporter of Gorbachev's reforms, but he was even more of a liberalizing zealot; he had earlier risen to the heights of Soviet power, but was pushed out in 1987 for arguing that reforms were not moving fast enough. Party insiders worried about the future of the Soviet state.

In August 1991, hardline communist politicians attempted a coup to oust the reformers. They took control of elements of the armed forces and forced their way into key government buildings with tanks, artillery, and special forces troops. But soldiers were forced back by civilian protestors led by Yeltsin, who held up in the parliament building, the White House, which became the focus of all opposition as coup leaders detained Gorbachev at his vacation home. When the dust settled, Yeltsin was the hero of the day. He began to be seen as the leader Russia needed, one who could lead the country towards a brighter future, separated both from the shackles of the institutions of the USSR and the rigid political ideology of communism.

Soon after the coup, the Soviet Union began to crumble. Gorbachev resigned as head of the Party, which shuttered. Ten republics seceded from the Soviet Union, and many gained foreign recognition. Even communist regimes abroad, like Angola, Ethiopia, and Cambodia, cast off Marxist institutions as the system was proven untenable in its birthplace.

On December 8, Yeltsin met in Belarus with leaders of former Soviet republics and declared what was now obvious to all: that the Soviet Union was dead. Gorbachev, he who instigated the reforms and then lost control of them, was thrust into the background. On December 15, he resigned as president of the USSR after declaring the formation of the Russian Federation in the place of the RSFSR, with Yeltsin as its new president. In his farewell address, Gorbachev observed, "The old system collapsed before the new one had time to start working."

THE COMMUNIST EXPERIMENT was over, shattered and cast off, like the statues of Lenin being torn down and discarded in overgrown back lots. The ideology that was supposed to reshape the world had been defeated, crushed by its own ponderous weight, unable to make one more step forward as the world around it spun out of its reach. For 69 years, 1922-1991, the Soviet Union had stood as the great counterpoint to the liberal, capitalist, democratic hegemony. No longer. Russia was now sailing into uncharted waters, rejoining a world it had exited in 1917.

Yeltsin, holding a traditional Russian flag rather than a communist one, rallying supporters during the August 1991 coup attempt. Image from the Press Office of the President of Russia.

Today, more than 30 years have passed since the fall of the USSR, more than enough time for it to gather a national mythos among Russians. It might seem that Russians would be anticommunists to a man, having slogged through nearly seven decades of a totalitarian police state. But no. Instead, today many Russians are nostalgic for the USSR – as much as 75 percent, according to one 2020 study.[81] The proportion echoes the March 1991 referendum results.

Older Russians grew up in the Soviet world of order, patriotism, and pride. The USSR had a clear national ideology with a unifying ethos. And many younger Russians see the Soviet period as a high point in Russia's history, when things were straightforward and the world feared Russia's might. A new Russian Communist Party was formed in 1993, two years after the Soviet Party was disbanded, and it remains one of the largest political parties active in the country. The hammer and sickle still adorn many public spaces, like metro stations and administration buildings. These are not relics of a shameful history; there is no sense of revulsion spurring their dismantling. They are instead the vestiges of a utopia that was within reach but just did not pan out.

For all its faults, the USSR was powerful, proud, and sure of itself. It was unharried by insidious outside influence and free to do what was in its best interest. The international community was scared to bully it. The implication: this is not the case today.

---

81. *Moscow Times*, "75% of Russians Say Soviet Era Was 'Greatest Time' in Country's History – Poll."

11

RE-LEGITIMIZATION: AFTER THE END OF HISTORY
Not totally new | Capitalism, almost | Democracy, almost | Georgia, Ukraine, and other diversions | Putinmania and its discontents

With the fall of the Soviet Union, some scholars welcomed the "end of history." The chief communist state had capitulated. Liberal democracy had scored a decisive win. All that remained was ever-increasing comfort, security, and profitability.

But for Russia, turning away from communism cast it, rudderless, onto a turbulent sea, and it was not clear where it would land. Yet, just as the seeds for the Soviet totalitarian state were planted in the turbulent years of the Revolution and Civil War, the upheaval of the post-Soviet period forged a new Russian state: one that, rather than joining the democratic, free-market order, has backed more and more into its own corner. This isolation has not been a punishment. Instead, it has been a goal, a source of pride, a sanctuary for the Russian state.

Inside the hollow shell created by the end of the USSR, today's Russia has re-legitimized itself, building a new nation founded on a new ideology: Putinism.

WHEN THE USSR became the Russian Federation in late 1991, it did not change overnight. In fact, much of it remained the same. The former communist Boris Yeltsin was still president. The Soviet congresses that governed the RSFSR simply became the higher and lower legislative houses of the Russian Senate and Russian State Duma, but with no subservience to an overarching Communist Party or USSR. The armed forces kept most of their structure, soldiers, and equipment, often even retaining their Soviet flags, patches, and roundels. Moscow remained the capital, and the Kremlin was still the site of supreme executive power. Many of the newly independent former republics that had stuck close to Russia through the Soviet period, like Kazakhstan and Belarus, joined a new Russia-led transnational organization, the Commonwealth of Independent States (CIS). Russia inherited the Soviet Union's seat at the United Nations. Even the national anthem stayed the same, just with a few key words changed.

Yet other aspects were updated, occasionally reverting all the way back to tsarist times. The double-headed eagle was reinstated as the official seal of the Russian Federation, hastily replacing the hammer and sickle on many landmarks, even in the Kremlin. The Russian flag went back to the banner of the late imperial period, with stripes of red, white, and blue.

Leningraders held a referendum to have the city's name changed back to St. Petersburg. Nicholas II and his family, the final Romanovs, were canonized as Orthodox saints and martyrs. Their remains were recovered and interred in a special chapel in the Peter and Paul Fortress, the hallowed burial place for the tsars since Peter the Great's day.

Western political and economic leaders saw great opportunity in this new Russia. The country had been thrust open and was fertile ground for new investment. Now was their chance to bring the former USSR – with all its resources for so long trapped behind an iron curtain and unable to be exploited – into the fold of the insatiable global capitalist beast, which was fresh off years of radical free-market leaders like Ronald Reagan and Margaret Thatcher. To add Russia's capital power to the global world order, experts advised what came to be called "shock therapy": rapid overhauls that would restructure the economy into a free-market system with few government regulations. It might take time for the market to stabilize, they argued, but in the end, Russia would have an economy on par with the finest anywhere. President Yeltsin, eager to bring Russia into a modern political economy interconnected with the Western superpowers, agreed to the plan.

The first question was what to do with all those enterprises under state control, all the plants, utilities, and services in which Russia's population worked. Now that the country was embracing free markets, these industries had to be subject to private ownership. The government, therefore, issued "shares" to individual citizens and auctioned off hundreds of enterprises to anyone able to pay in the shares. But the very act of auctioning off these profitable businesses to the highest bidder betrayed a flaw: those with the wherewithal to accumulate shares or to manipulate enterprise finances and boards were usually former Communist Party members with prior political and monetary influence. They and their families were insiders before, and insiders they would stay, creating a new class of aristocrats. The personal patronage networks of the Soviet age thus lived on, only now clad in tailored business suits from Savile Row.

Now that businesses were in private hands, industries could consolidate. Lack of competition and basic communist ideology had led to inefficiencies in the Soviet economy: everyone was guaranteed a job and a living wage, even if the company operated at a loss. But now, extra factories and redundant projects had to be shut down to save the bottom line, so workers were laid off. Those operations that still worked faced such a poor domestic economy that even employed Russians missed out on months of paychecks. Problems were exacerbated by rising prices, inflation, and stubborn corruption. Alcoholism and suicide rates in Russia rose to among the highest in the world. The birth rate was so low that the overall population declined. Crime spiked as people became desperate, and police were paid so little that many took side jobs or only worked when bribed. To protect their assets, many wealthy individuals and new businessmen hired economically vulnerable Russians as bodyguards and underlings, further fostering the oligarch class.

At the same time, thousands of wealthy and educated Russians left the country for the West, caused a brain drain. What little wealth did enter Russia stayed in the glitzy cosmopolitan centers of St. Petersburg and Moscow, in the hands of the new elite class and their circles. Russian society's new trajectory was radically different from the one of only a few years prior. What Russia had gotten in return for selling its soul was not prosperity but destitution. And it was the common people who paid the price most dearly.[82]

But still Yeltsin stayed the course, committed to political and economic liberalism, certain benefits were just around the corner. In September 1993, unable to push his agenda through an increasingly independent and intransigent legislature, the president illegally dissolved the Duma and moved to strengthen the presidential office. For his opponents, this was both a constitutional crisis and the last straw. Thousands marched on government buildings in Moscow, occupying the White House once again. Now it was Yeltsin's turn to crack down, sending in troops and ordering tanks to fire on the building. Hundreds were killed and wounded. After nearly two weeks, order was restored. The Duma lived on, but the Russian presidency was attracting more power.

But, nagged by both economic and political turmoil, the new Russia was emasculated and embarrassed. What had once been the great counterbalance of the West, the other great power, able to strike fear into the heart of the White House, full of military might, was now an impoverished country with little hope for a better future. This was not helped by bungled military farces in separatist regions of the Caucasus, where local leaders seeking independence were quashed only after great difficulty and loss of life. Watchers in the West feared a return to communism. For the everyday Russian, for whom the promises of capitalism had failed to materialize, a return to communist certainty would have been appealing.

Through it all, Yeltsin clung doggedly to the presidency. Rubbing elbows with the most powerful men of his day, Yeltsin stayed in the good graces of leaders as a friend to the West who was doing his darndest to bring Russia into the liberal-democratic fold. In 1995, he engineered another sell-off of state assets, this time heavily favoring the oligarch class. The scheme successfully raised money for Yeltsin's 1996 re-election campaign and further contributed to the consolidation of power among an exclusive elite. Over the next four years, Yeltsin's health and approval rating plummeted. Neither was helped by his frequent drinking. Difficult leadership took its toll.

ON NEW YEAR'S Eve 1999, Yeltsin officially resigned and turned the presidency over to the recently elected prime minister, a certain Vladimir Putin, an unknown figure to much of the public. With a speech from the new head of state televised nation-wide, the Kremlin clock struck midnight. Russia entered the 21st century with Putin at the helm.

Putin's biography is hard to pin down. His life has been distorted by Putin himself as well as his regime, spinning and embellishing as needed. We know that he was born in St. Petersburg

---

82. For fascinating looks at the effects and legacy of the 1990s in Russia, see Garrels, *Putin Country*.

in 1952. His grandfather was reputedly a cook for Lenin and Stalin.[83] Putin claims poverty and a rough childhood: according to the official story, as a kid, he had to fight off rats in the streets while scrounging for scraps. From a young age, he expressed interest in joining the KGB, the infamous Soviet spy agency of the Cold War. However, unable to apply, he learned German and was eventually recruited. He spent most of his time stationed in Dresden, East Germany. He could have been a secret agent agitating for the communist cause in the Eastern Bloc, but evidence points to him more likely being a liaison officer. In the 1990s, Putin left the KGB[84] and joined the administrative staff of the local St. Petersburg government. There, he was accused of foreign aid corruption but evaded an investigation. In 1997, he leveraged his connections to land a job as President Yeltsin's chief of staff in Moscow, rising through the ranks and gaining additional responsibility, eventually becoming prime minister. After less than a year in that position, Yeltsin handed Putin the Kremlin keys and retired.

Putin was a young-looking 47 when he took office, youthful compared to the septuagenarian Yeltsin and the gray-haired communist leaders that had preceded him. In addition, Putin's KGB credentials and extensive history of government service marked him as someone who had participated in and believed in the Soviet system but still had the Russian people's best interests at his core. Even today, as Putin enters his seventies and the length of his tenure in power inches ever closer to the record set by Stalin (29 years), many in the public continue to see him as a safe choice for the post-Soviet millennium.

President Putin got right to work after his appointment to the presidency. In his first years in office, he did two things that immediately solidified his rule. First, he squelched insurgents in the Caucasian province of Chechnya. By installing a friendly puppet to lead the province and providing a level of nominal autonomy, he was able to bring the region into the Russian fold and ensure its loyalty moving forward. Then he invested heavily in the oil and natural gas industries. By tapping into these natural resources and tying the value of Russian currency to the price of oil, Russia was able to take advantage of the early-2000s fossil fuel boom and profit off the wild gas-guzzling consumerism of the West.

Concurrently, several industries were brought back under state control, most critically Russia's largest financial and energy institutions. Wealthy oligarchs, rather than being gangsters, were brought into the government and given important industrial posts in newly re-nationalized companies, granting them legitimate forms of income while at the same time helping Putin secure his power and fostering connections with leaders of domestic industry. This also encouraged the funneling of huge sums of cash towards Putin himself and a growing network of allies and clients.

---

83. One story relates that Vladimir's granddad, Spiridon Putin, once bumped into Grigory Rasputin at a swanky St. Petersburg hotel. Rasputin was so charmed by the similarity of their names that he gave Spiridon a golden ruble. The tale is impossible to verify.

84. But, in Putin's own immortal words, "There's no such thing as a former KGB man."

A fresh-faced Putin takes his first oath of office as president of the Russian Federation, January 2000, as an aging Yeltsin looks on. From the Press Office of the President of Russia.

The Russian economy first stabilized, then exploded, and the standard of living greatly improved. It deftly weathered economic downturns that crippled the U.S., Asia, and Europe in the early 2000s. The booming market allowed for more robust social programs, such as pensions for the elderly and fiscal support for children and young families. A close association with a resurgent Orthodox Church was reforged, accepting a responsibility to educate the masses and help pass along traditional Russian values that served a patriotic purpose and discouraged dissent. Moscow's massive outdoor pool was reconverted back into a soaring cathedral to replicate the original, with financial support from affluent oligarchs, Putin's regime, and the Church.

All this led to soaring support for the new president. It appeared that Putin had proven to be just the right man for the job.

Putin's popularity won him reelection in 2004 for his second term. But here a problem arose: the Russian constitution forbade him a third term in 2008-12. No matter; for that period, Putin's ally and prime minister Dmitri Medvedev took power to buy time while the law was changed to allow for Putin to return to power and stay there. He returned to the presidency in 2012 and has been there ever since. Thanks to more constitutional changes in recent years, Putin is now legally able to be Russia's president until 2036, when he will be 83, surpassing Stalin's record by six years.

Putin's actions, even from early on in his tenure, fit neither into the hard-left matrix of communism nor in the free-market liberalism of Yeltsin and the wider West. Putin supports a broadly conservative agenda that is hard to categorize neatly into a Western policy paradigm of right or left. The unique blend of an economy integrated with the state apparatus, with concurrent robust social programs, all tied together by radical patriotism, has been coined "Putinism." But what exactly Putinism is – and whether it is an ideology or simply a pragmatic and cynical tool intended solely to preserve executive power and accumulate obscene wealth – has been the subject of intense debate.

Putinism is not intrinsically anti-democratic. After his initial appointment to the presidency, Putin has been democratically elected each time he has held office (or at least he has made an effort to appear to be democratically elected). There are active political parties besides United Russia, the one Putin heads, such as the Communist Party, Liberal Democratic Party, and the Just Russia Party, but these often work alongside United Russia and rarely put up much meaningful resistance. Outside observers are often tempted to label this "fascism." But this is simplistic, and Russians would reject this comparison vehemently.[85]

Putinism had ripples far from Russia's borders, too. Russia in effect rejected the free market democracy the West offered and instead turned towards an authoritarian "third way." And the turn has worked out magnificently.

Not long after his rise to power, Putin and his administration began to use patriotic rhetoric that sounded strikingly militant. Western fears of Russian incursion, which had cooled after the end of the Cold War, were rekindled. Russia's neighbors sought protection, fearing that Putin might invade to reclaim land (and clout) lost in the late 20th century. NATO and other international military and economic organizations continued to add Eastern European nations to their rosters as attack by Russia became an increasing threat.

Even former Soviet states, those that were members of the USSR with close ties to Moscow, broke ranks. Political debates in many former Soviet states became dominated by the merits of continuing to embrace Russian leadership or making a pivot to the West, perhaps even joining the European Union. A series of "color revolutions," so called because pro-democracy activists color-coordinated their demonstrations in capitals, rocked post-Soviet nations, like the Rose Revolution in Georgia (2003), the Yellow Revolution in Mongolia (2005), and the Orange Revolution in Ukraine (2005-06). Russia has painted these as Western provocations, covert acts to turn its longtime friends against it. In response, Russia has often seen fit to send in troops. Sometimes, this has resulted in "frozen conflicts," wherein a stalemate ensues that cripples the invaded nation while hardly affecting Russia. This happened in Moldova in 1991, Georgia in 2008, and Ukraine in 2014. In all of these cases, the frozen conflict has hampered the defender's ability to liberalize and join the West while also confirming Russian power by flexing its muscle abroad.

---

85. Those interested can start with any of the following: Giles, *Moscow Rules*; Robinson, *Russian Conservatism*; and Laruelle, *Is Russia Fascist?* The summary here is merely the tip of the iceberg.

In turn, Russia's aggressive international actions have led to waves of sanctions from the West over the past 25 years. These usually sought to target oligarchs and the Russian state, but often it was Russian citizens who were hit with higher prices or inaccessibility to foreign goods. Thus, while the assertion of Russian power at home and abroad has made the Russian people more confident and has legitimized Putin as president, at the same time it has sharply driven Russia away from Western institutions.

Still, Russia continues its march under Putin, proud, yet perhaps with some lingering insecurity. Some dissenters have challenged the regime, with little success. Boris Nemtsov, a liberal politician who was a critic of Putin's belligerence, was brazenly assassinated just below the Kremlin walls on the night of February 27, 2015. More recently, Alexey Navalny, an internet-powered anticorruption lawyer and activist who posted YouTube videos detailing the nefarious business schemes of Putin and his cronies, was poisoned in August 2021, then evacuated from Russia to Germany to recover.

While there, Navalny and his organization released a two-hour-long YouTube video investigating a gaudy, mysterious palace on the Black Sea that could only belong to Putin himself. Peppered with irreverent humor and bolstered by a thorough investigation, the video, as of early 2025, has over 130 million views. Putin has officially and repeatedly denied ownership of the palace, with its stripper poles, video game rooms, ice-hockey rink, wine cellar, and perplexingly-titled "aquadiskoteka."[86] The president insisted that it belongs to a Russian businessman, but Navalny's video argued otherwise. According to the investigation, the getaway was funded through grift that could only be collected by someone at the highest levels of decades of systematic corruption.

When Navalny returned to Russia in January 2021, he was immediately arrested on vague charges of "extremism" and sent to prison. He died under mysterious circumstances, still incarcerated, in February 2024. He was perhaps Putin's most outspoken critic in Russia. Since then, no one has risen to take his place.

Russia under Putin continues to search for a new identity.

TODAY, RUSSIA IS the world's largest country in the world by area, stretching from the warm shores of Crimea (if you ignore Ukraine's claim) to the remote forests of Sakhalin Island (if you ignore Japan's claim). St. Petersburg remains the nation's historic heart, with architecture, canals, and museums that drew millions of annual visitors from around the world before travel effectively ceased. Moscow is still the capital, with some 20 million living in it and its environs, placing it among the largest cities in Europe. And both cities are bursting with newfound wealth, with pristine new business districts that have appeared since Putin took the helm.

But look behind the veneer, and all is not as rosy as it may seem. In a problem that has harried Russia for hundreds of years, many of the provinces have been left behind. Post-

---

86. Navalny, "Putin's Palace."

Putin's palace (alleged), an aerial view. In the foreground, a fake hill covers a full-size hockey rink; next to it are two helipads. Gardens lead to the main house. Behind it is the swimming pool and "aquadiskoteka," overlooking the Black Sea. Other outbuildings include guest houses, an amphitheater, and wine-tasting pavilions. From Alexey Navalny's YouTube channel.

industrial towns, like the medieval center of Novgorod, are still struggling to find their place in a post-Soviet Russia that once fuelled them and gave them purpose. Many villages far from cities are still without electricity; some estimates say that 20 percent of Russians don't have access to indoor plumbing.[87]

If Navalny was correct, Putin is the richest man on Earth, by far. His country? One of economic inequality and stubborn pockets of poverty, powered by the export of oil and little else. And, since its full-scale invasion of Ukraine in 2022, Russia has become an international outcast, heavily sanctioned and effectively cut off from the outside world. The ongoing military operation has led to crackdowns on dissent reminiscent of the worst of tsarist and Soviet times. Putin grows older by the day, and more and more it seems like Russia has been remade in his image; an opposition-free, tyrannical image.

So here we are.

---

87. Moscow Times, "Indoor Plumbing."

12

INTERPRETATION: TODAY'S RUSSIAN PAST
New history | Themes and methods | Tying it all together

It is not Russian history that is critical to understanding modern Russia, although it does help to provide a foundation. Rather, it is *how that history is retold* that builds a collective memory, from which springs a unified nation. To support the state's ends, the Russian past presented today is molded and manipulated in specific, intentional ways.

When the Putin regime came to power, officials had to write a fresh history, one that dovetailed smoothly onto the values Putin promoted but that also cemented his power. The tsarist retelling was no longer relevant, and the Marxist hermeneutic was shattered in 1991. But the quasi-ideology of Putinism has doggedly massaged Russian history to present a careful narrative that supports policies and practices of the state.

This history can be glimpsed in multiple places, but two stand out.

First, in 2018, the Russian foreign minister, Sergei Lavrov, published an essay, "Russian Foreign Policy in a Historical Perspective," in which he highlighted specific historical events and asserted their importance for informing modern Russian international relations. Lavrov argued that Russian history, and wider world history, should be approached from a lens that emphasizes continuity. In his words, "A well thought-out policy cannot be detached from history."[88] And so the past, specifically the past as told by modern Russia, must necessarily inform the present; events from hundreds of years ago can be said, essentially, to have happened to the modern Russian state.

Second, a recent history exhibition called "Russia: My History," which began in Moscow and later spread to more than two dozen satellite sites in cities around Russia, gave the Russian state free reign to present a narrative lens to its people, especially children. The exhibition gives the whole of Russia's story through interactive multimedia displays, marrying fact and narrative with interpretation, informing visitors how historical episodes ought to be interpreted. The theme of continuity is emphasized once again, in the very name of the project, once more emphasizing how important history is to the Russian conception of self.

---

88. Lavrov, "Russian Foreign Policy in a Historical Perspective."

If we want to understand why Russia is like it is, why it behaves as it does, sources like these are two invaluable places to look.[89] They are comprehensive narratives directly from the Kremlin.

These sources and others from the Russian state show us that there are three significant themes in the Kremlin's retelling of Russian history, and these themes are the bedrock of the Putinist worldview. By emphasizing these aspects of the past, the modern state claims certain values and propagates them for the future.

These themes are:
- the value of strong leaders;
- Russia as the Third Rome perpetually under siege; and
- the need for constant wariness and creative defense against foreign influence.

These themes do not exist as neat, separate entities; rather, they interact and reinforce one another. Each deserves a close look.

STRONG LEADERS. According to the official narrative, the most dramatic positive changes in Russian history came about through individuals. It was Vladimir I who baptized the Rus' and jumpstarted its unique Orthodox culture. It was Ivan III who unified the Russian cities, Ivan IV who centralized the state. Peter I and Catherine II modernized Russia into a European power. Lenin led the Revolution, and Stalin harnessed Soviet industry to defeat the Nazis. Putin made Russia great again. These are just a few examples of tsars, princes, and general secretaries who, for all their faults, got things done.

A strong leader could make Russia unequalled in power. The lack of one, as in the Time of Troubles or the late Soviet period, could bring it to the brink of extinction. The right person at the right time makes all the difference. The prototypical Russian leader is the one that is most tyrannical, but also the most decisive. He cuts through red tape and checks and balances to govern effectively, to his people's benefit. Per the Kremlin, effective, unilateral autocracy has historically been the rule for good governance in the Russian context.

Here the Westerner pauses; chances are, they are skeptical of powerful leaders because they are, by definition, despotic. Much of the modern West, especially the United States, is founded on ideas of limited government and skepticism of those in power, with the mandate to rule in the hands of the people and agency dispersed through checks and balances. Objections arise naturally: How many Russians were baptized against their will? How many serfs were killed in the construction of St. Petersburg? How many Ukrainians starved thanks to Stalin's economic policy? Were those lurching leaps in progress based on a tsar's or Soviet leader's whim really worth it? Absolutely, responds the Russian state. Necessary, even. What are a few lives when the future of Russia itself is at stake? If Russia is great today, it is because of the decisions of its all-powerful, confident, ambitious rulers. Those who suffered did so for a noble cause.

---

89. A good secondary source that discusses modern Moscow's take on Russia's history, especially in light of Ukraine, is Plokhy, *Lost Kingdom*.

Visitors to Russia have long suspected, and sociological studies have confirmed, that Russians tend to view strong leaders favorably.[90] And it should be no surprise that Putin, having made himself an autocrat, deliberately embraces the strong-leader archetype. A St. Petersburg native, he identifies closely with Peter the Great, finding parallels between Peter's modernization and his own efforts to shoulder Russia's way back to world-power status in the 21st century.[91] Hence also the extreme care Putin puts into his masculine self-image, sometimes to comedic effect, as when photographed shirtless on a horse or diving for ancient amphorae. And if Putin has become fabulously wealthy and powerful thanks to his position, well, at least Russia is doing better now than it was before him. He has earned it, the argument goes.

In recent years, though, some in Russia itself have begun to bring a certain skepticism to this historical theme. This was the case in May 2019, when a newly-unveiled Stalin statue in Novosibirsk was met with emotional responses from two extremes: enthusiastic support and disgusted denunciation.[92] Similarly the case with Ivan IV, whose Oryol statue, erected with Putin's blessing and the endorsement of the Church, was parodied with a "bloody" wooden stake in the Far East city of Kansk. These instances imply that the unilateral view of strong leaders as a positive aspect of Russian society was already shifting in the years leading up to the invasion of Ukraine.

Yet the traditional Russian desire for strong leadership pulls just as strong, if not more forcefully. Even as thousands of young people attended rallies for the dissident activist Alexei Navalny, as they did across the Federation after his arrest, the majority of Russians shrugged and went on with their lives, confident in and content with Putin, who regularly pulls in ever-larger crowds at speaking events and has for decades. And any hint of a liberalizing trend has dried up in the wake of Russia's invasion of Ukraine. As of late 2024, public numbers indicated that nearly three-quarters of Russians support Putin, with no decrease in 2025.[93] Even if the statistic is exaggerated, with that level of approval, the president has a blank check to remain the central figure of Russian society for years to come.

RUSSIA AS THE BESIEGED THIRD ROME. With Putin's rise to power, the myth of Russia as the Third Rome has seen a forceful resurgence. The Third Rome idea was alive and well during the Imperial period, but, in the atheistic Soviet era, it was supplanted by a new Great Commission: to go and make communists of all nations. Today, however, the Third Rome narrative has been rehabilitated and is alive and well, revived for the post-Soviet world. It has provided a new raison d'être to Russia, its leaders, and its people.

---

90. Chiozza and Stoyanov. "The Myth of the Strong Leader in Russian Public Opinion."

91. Glasser, "Putin the Great."

92. Hartog, "Is Stalin Making a Comeback in Russia?"

93. Edwards, "Putin Still Popular"; Edwards, "Putin's Popularity Perpetuates."

To review, the Third Rome myth argues that Russia has a sacred mission to carry on the true form of Christianity (Orthodoxy, literally "right belief") for the rest of the world, no matter what the cost, and must therefore be guarded zealously from the secular, godless powers seeking to overtake it. Apologists argue that Russia is the inheritor of the sacred Roman Empire by way of its baptism into Byzantine culture and religion. The argument cites close ties between Constantinople and medieval Russia in terms of trade, politics, and culture, manifested in Ivan III's marriage to the niece of the last Byzantine emperor. Today's Russian state seal once more bears the ancient Byzantine double-headed eagle, and modern Russian culture is inextricably tied to Eastern Orthodox religion and culture. According to Navalny's famed video, the double-headed eagle even adorns the front gates of Putin's Black Sea vacation home.

In Moscow's retelling, the fact that Russia has repeatedly survived past invasions against the odds feeds into the notion that it is divinely ordained to persist. The most notable attacks came from the Mongols in the 13th century, Poland in the 17th, France in the 19th, and Germany in the 20th. In each instance, the narrative has it, Russia returned with a vengeance, preserving its Orthodox religion, freedom, and way of life when other nations would have folded. Russia has always been under siege by those outside, who are jealous of its wealth and standing, but God, with His eyes always on Russia, has consistently protected it.

In modern times, this narrative takes on a new meaning. For one, in the 20th and 21st centuries, Russia's enemies wear different clothes. Whereas the historical invaders came at Russia with swords, warhorses, and tanks, more recently, godless bankers, policymakers, and civil society puppetmasters work behind the scenes to subvert Russia for political gain and plunder it for monetary gain. After all, in the 1990s, Russia was humiliated by its enemies as they kicked it while it was down, just as happened in the Time of Troubles or when the Nazis broke the Molotov-Ribbentrop Pact in 1941. The names have changed, but the West has always been, and always will be, eager to backstab at the first opportunity. There exists a persistent conspiracy against Holy Russia everywhere you look, and that is the way it has always been. Russians must be on their guard, always.

What does the West want, according to Russia? Nothing short of the implementation of the philosophies of neoliberalism in Russia. Callous free markets. Atheism, or at least apathy towards religion. A neutered state and army. Dissent and disorder. Cynical critiques of a patriotic past. Unruly youth. Effeminate men. Foreigners crowding out indigenous Russians. Women forgoing children for economic advancement. The Kremlin looks at America in the 2020s and from it produces an apocalyptic picture, vowing not to let themselves become like that by indulging in weak pleasures. They pledge instead to hew close to the traditional Orthodox way of life: manliness, militarism, and unwavering unity with your countrymen and support for your nation. Thus Russia has in recent years implemented sweeping programs to promote child-rearing among young families, forbidden LGBT displays, cracked down on abortion, and deported thousands of immigrants back to their home countries. All the things the West is not, Russia must be.[94]

For an explicit example of how this ideology is presented, there is the Russian Orthodox Church's 2012 documentary on the 1453 fall of Constantinople, "The Fall of an Empire." The parallel, which is ham-fisted and obvious, is that Russia is very much like mid-15th-century Constantinople, and the Turks are very much like the West. Constantinople is strong when it promotes national pride, remains pious and religiously upright, and sticks to its traditional ways. When it compromises on its values, allowing in unscrupulous moneychangers and those promoting homosexual promiscuity, it becomes vulnerable to its enemies and is betrayed by its allies, whose only principles are greed and personal advancement at the detriment of others. The message, endorsed by the Kremlin and its religious allies, is clear: Russia must strictly abide in its pious exceptionalism, lest it fall.

In April 2020, with the spread of COVID-19 to Russia (which tore through the country thanks to a bumbling response from the Kremlin, devastating its population worse than almost anywhere else on earth), Putin galvanized his people by saying, "Everything passes and this too will pass. Our country has been through serious tests more than once: When tormented by the Pechenegs and the Cumans, Russia coped with everything."[95] Why he chose two relatively obscure premodern nomadic invaders from the times of Kievan Rus' rather than something more modern (and more relatable) is a mystery, but it once more highlights the point. Russia still sees itself as eternally threatened by external forces. However, through uniquely Russian grit and the blessing of God for His Third Rome, it has the ability to deftly navigate and, when push comes to shove, defend itself from insidious invaders.

PARANOIA AND PREPARATION. If Russia is the sacred Third Rome, constantly stalked by dark forces and under perpetual threat, then a response to this threat is justified. But simply resisting the Goliath of liberal ideals will not suffice. There is always tension, war can break out at any moment, and it never hurts to be prepared, even proactive. The West is probably already plotting Russia's destruction. We must think of those heroes that rose to the occasion: Nevsky, Minin and Pozharsky, Ivan Susanin, your own grandparents and great-grandparents fighting the Nazis and Whites. They took on the challenge to fight for Russia. According to the Kremlin narrative, all should look for opportunities not to divide into internal factions, but to unify and follow in our ancestors' footsteps.

This means that, for the sake of safety, any dissent can be quickly quashed. After all, anti-regime protests are essentially anti-Russia protests, making their participants traitors by definition, no matter the issue. Further, they are probably funded by the insidious and embittered West in a colonialist effort to cripple Russia. This paranoia, coupled with a lack

---

94. Graeber and Wengrow, in *The Dawn of Everything*, call this "schismogenesis," whereby cultures define themselves as the antithesis of neighboring cultures. The term is certainly applicable here.

95. Edwards, "Meet Russia's Newest Meme: Pechenegs."

of a political heritage that curtails government oppression and surveillance, means that, even today, those who rock the boat can find themselves under watch, in legal trouble, or simply dead. With so many threats outside, trust of the state and its institutions is almost a Russian value in and of itself, and patriotism (in other words, exceptional Third Rome "Russian-ness") must be constantly and tenaciously promoted and reinforced. Since Russia stands to lose its very existence, any measure is on the table.

Often, modern Russia does this through what some scholars call "sharp power." Whereas hard power entails military or economic coercion, and soft power is actions through diplomacy, cultural exchange, and persuasion, sharp power refers to state-funded activities that promote a government and an affinity for its culture in foreign territories through nonmilitary means. It is directed and deliberate soft power for goals usually accomplished with hard power.[96] Historically, and unlike many Western countries, the Russian state allows for the close cooperation of the Kremlin, church, businesses, and cultural institutions, making sharp power an easy thing to promote. All of these can be mobilized together and leveraged for their strengths to achieve specific goals.

There are several examples of sharp power in action within and without Russia, and these examples take many forms. Most obvious are Moscow-funded but internationally-broadcast television and news agencies, like Russia Today and Russia Beyond. Russia Today (RT) is an official-looking news agency that reports on current events, invariably through a pro-Russia filter that demonizes the West and treats Russia as an ever-besieged victim. The website Russia Beyond is a little lighter and more subtle fare, like a Russia-themed Buzzfeed, but it is also run by the Kremlin. Articles might dive into celebrations of Russian culture or factoids on historical Russian military practice. But at their core these are simply propaganda tools, leftover from the days of the USSR, except now YouTube, TikTok, and Twitter/X provide a much larger reach than covert radio waves or the Red Army Choir ever could.

On the more bizarre side are projects like the Night Wolves, a pro-Putin ultranationalist biker gang.[97] Funded by the Russian Ministry of Culture, the club embodies an image of scofflaw masculinity and performs youth-friendly displays of motocross talent throughout Russia. Shows draw parallels between modern Ukraine, NATO, and the United States with Nazi Germany. They feature rousing songs, flamboyant patriotic images, daredevil motorbike stunts, and stunning pyrotechnics. The leader of the Night Wolves is Alexander Zaldostanov, a former surgeon. He has received medals for his service to the Motherland as well as obsequious praise from Putin himself for shaping the Russian youth of tomorrow. As wild as it is, the Night Wolves' displays and manly antics are merely tools for spreading pro-Russian sentiment both at home and abroad.

---

96. See Walker, "What Is 'Sharp Power'?"

97. Edwards, "Biking with Style, with Putin."

With the very fabric of Russian society on the line, any measure of sharp power is acceptable. Often, the goal of sharp power is simply to cause chaos and sow distrust, and any American who remembers the 2016 and 2020 presidential races will recall just how effective Russian ploys were in achieving that. But to the Kremlin, these are workaday tools to help defend the sacred Russian nation from insidious outside influence.

These, then, are the inner logic, ideology, and methods of Putinism in a nutshell. Putin's framework combines these three key aspects of the Russian historical narrative to shore up the Kremlin's power in any way possible. It is an amalgamation of nationalistic, right-wing, conservative, pro-social-support, pro-religion narratives. Policy-wise, it offers pragmatic solutions that have served not only to empower and enrich Putin himself but have also kept the Russian public largely compliant, or at least silenced.

Most crucially, Putinism is deeply, inextricably rooted in the Russian past. This is why it is so difficult to pin down when looking from the outside in with little context. Under Putinism, history is a weapon, a tool of oppression, a servant of the exceptional Russian state. As much as history informs ideology, at the same time, ideology influences a specific reading of history. Even today, we see shadows of Peter the Great, Ivan IV, Lenin, the debate between Slavophiles and Westernizers, and the tsarist mantra of "Orthodoxy, Autocracy, Nationality."

Therefore, understanding and interpreting Russian history is the single best avenue to understanding why the country acts as it does.

The full-scale Russian invasion of Ukraine has made understanding Russian history, and its meaning, more critical than ever. Since the first offensive in February 2022, the Russian president has only further ensconced himself in his historical retelling, doubling down on Putinist revisionism to justify his actions. For many in the West, the war continues to puzzle. However, equipped with the themes of the Kremlin's history, it is possible to untangle.

Putin hangs out with members of the Night Wolves biker club, 2019. An image published by the Press Office of the President of Russia.

13

APPLICATION: UKRAINE

Quod erat demonstrandum | Parallel history | Casus belli? | Today | Tomorrow

Russia's full-scale invasion of Ukraine threw Putinism into the spotlight. It showed how Putinism's take on Russian history could be worked out on the world stage. Further, much of the rhetoric about Ukraine, the language used to justify the conflict and convince Russian citizens and the world that Russia is in the right, has come from the past. The invasion is a case-in-point for how Russia is using a specific retelling of the past to promote certain values and frame certain questions in an effort to gain and maintain power.

In short, Russia's war on Ukraine has been ground zero for the recasting of Russia's modern history. The ideology of Putinism has been given full expression, and its specific retelling of the past has only come to light more brightly.

From the Western point of view, the origins of the Ukraine conflict are unclear and convoluted, even among experts. When conservative American pundit Tucker Carlson interviewed Putin, many in the West were confused. Even journalists struggled to make heads or tails of the obscure references to long-dead historical figures and dismissed Putin's historical excuses as "nonsense."[98] One step from confusion is the temptation to simply dismiss Russian culture as devoid of value and the Russian state as inherently corrupt and evil.[99] This is neither justified nor helpful. Instead, we should note the consistency in the Kremlin's messaging, one that takes form in light of the context of Putinistic history and the values it enshrines.

The histories of Russia and Ukraine are closely intertwined. In the medieval period, Kievan Rus' had its heartland stretching from Kiev to near modern St. Petersburg, and it was in Ukraine's Crimean Peninsula that Vladimir the Great, a hero to both nations, was baptized. The region that makes up modern Ukraine was the site of much of the development of early Russian culture and art.

When the Mongols invaded, the Ukrainian lands remained in foreign control for much longer than northern areas. However, in the 17th and 18th centuries, much of western Ukraine,

---

98. Vock, "Tucker Carlson interview."

99. Edwards, "What is Russophobia?"

including the capital, Kiev, fell under the control of the Polish-Lithuanian Commonwealth. This exposed Kiev to Western thought, which at the time was wrestling with Catholic humanism and the Counter-Reformation, to a much greater extent than Moscow ever encountered it. Kiev became a major urban center under Polish rule; its university predates any in Russia, and its close proximity to the Black Sea meant that it was much more diverse than Russia at the time. Already, Ukrainian culture was growing distinct from Russian culture.

Only in the 18th century did campaigns by the Russian Empire make all of Ukraine into Imperial Russian territory. Much of eastern Ukraine was a sparsely-inhabited hinterland far from power centers. Indeed, the Russian word "Ukraine" derives from the word "*krai*," meaning edge.[100] Russian authorities termed the area "Novorossiya" ("New Russia") in an effort to encourage colonial-style settlement while also asserting an intrinsic right to the land.

Russia established a naval base on the Crimean Peninsula in the 19th century to project sea power into the Mediterranean, making it a target of other empires of the time, as during the Crimean War. Still, Ukrainian territory was more Western-looking and cosmopolitan than Russia proper, even as it was a constituent territory of the empire. Its western part had a large proportion of Catholics with ties to the West, and Black Sea ports attracted diverse, well-educated merchant classes of both Jewish and Turkish descent. Ukraine had its own language, closely related to Russian, but with influences from far afield. Many tongues could be heard in the melting-pot ports of the coast.

Following the 1917 Revolution, Ukraine became a separate republic in the USSR: the Ukrainian Soviet Socialist Republic. Under Stalin, millions of Ukrainians died in the Holodomor, a famine caused by poor implementation of agricultural reform and made worse by prioritizing grain for Russian citizens over Ukrainians. Into this population vacuum were sent Russian farmers, who took up land in eastern Ukraine's Donbass region, swinging its demographics Russia-ward.

When Nazi Germany invaded from the west, many Ukrainians opted to collude with the invading army. The choice between allegiance to Hitler's Nazi Germany and Stalin's Communist Russia was not an easy one, made even more complicated by the recent famine. Many Ukrainians likely thought that their odds for survival and prosperity were better with an outside regime hostile to Moscow and collaborated with the invaders. But to Moscow, this was an unforgivable sin.

Ukraine saw some of the heaviest fighting of the war, and the USSR was able to expel the Germans only after intense conflict and the devastation of much of the region. With the fall of the Soviet Union, Ukraine was eager to declare independence, with 91 percent of voters supporting independence in a December 1991 referendum. However, its ruling class maintained close ties to Russia, as many in power were former communist officials with

---

100. This etymology has created a grammatical shibboleth. In Russian, the prepositions "*v*," meaning "in," and "*na*," meaning "on," can both be used when saying something is "in" Ukraine. However, using "*v*" is more Ukraine-friendly, as it implies being "in" the borders of an independent, sovereign state, whereas using "*na*" implies being "on" the borderland of a large country (in this case, Russia).

friends in the Kremlin. Russia negotiated a lease on the Crimean naval base, territory it had kept through the Soviet period, but the rest of the republic formally passed out of Moscow's control. Its independence was undisputed.

In 2004, Russia-friendly politician Viktor Yanukovich was declared to be the winner of a presidential election that was largely suspected of being rigged. Ukrainians, furious at the outcome and suspecting Russian interference, protested by gathering in public spaces and wearing orange in support of the opposition candidate, Viktor Yushchenko. At the same time, Yushchenko fell severely and suspiciously ill. He recovered, although his face was scarred with pocks. This assassination attempt boosted his public image as a courageous martyr and propelled him into the presidential office when the election results were overturned.

In many ways, the "Orange Revolution" marked a step for Ukraine towards the West, as an opposition politician who was not pre-approved by Russia had taken power in Kiev. But complicating the picture is the fact that, while it has long been believed that Russian agents poisoned Yushchenko, it is also a near-certainty that Western agencies bankrolled the protestors and activists who supported him. What the West saw as an effort to evangelize democratic institutions to a new nation Russia saw as a plot to turn its relative, a member of its closest family, against it. Once again, the Third Rome was under attack by a wealthy, unscrupulous West.

Regardless, Yushchenko's regime was short-lived. The pro-Kremlin Yanukovich soon returned to the presidency, and for years Ukraine was caught in a tug-of-war between Russia and the West. This was until November 2013, when, against the popular will, Yanukovich shot down a deal that would have fostered closer ties with the European Union in favor of cozying up to Putin's Russia. Protestors took to Kiev's Maidan ("Freedom") Square, camping out for weeks and braving riot police, fires, and winter weather. It has been estimated that more than 100 protestors died in the demonstrations, almost solely due to police brutality by the pro-Russian regime. Finally, Yanukovich fled to Russia in February 2014. The Maidan Uprising was a signal that Ukraine was heading towards the West and possible integration into NATO or the EU.

But Russia was wary of having a close neighbor, one that shared such intricate historical, ideological, economic, and political ties, looking West. They suspected foul play. Surely the Maidan protests were engineered by Western elites – George Soros, Hillary Clinton, Bill Gates, and their ilk – in an attempt to humiliate Russia, to gain a pawn almost in its heartland. The Ukrainians would have to pay. The West would, too, someday.

The response was swift. As early as that February, unmarked troops began appearing on the Crimean Peninsula. These "little green men" with no national insignia surreptitiously secured key government buildings and military sites and claimed them for Russia. With Russian control almost solidified, officials in the Crimean Peninsula held a hasty referendum. A reported 98 percent of voters chose for the region to leave Ukraine and reunite with Russia.

Putin claimed that the Crimean people had made their voices heard and welcomed Crimea as a new Russian territory.

At the same time, two impoverished, industrial, Russian-ethnic-majority regions in Donbass, eastern Ukraine, declared themselves the independent Luhansk People's Republic and Donetsk People's Republic. Russia recognized these breakaway regions almost immediately. Conflict erupted between Ukrainian state forces and Russian-backed separatists in the area. While not explicitly parts of Russia, these areas fell under de facto rule of Moscow, which supplied them with troops, arms, and logistical support. Ukraine lost the territory but lacked the strength to counterattack. Both sides settled into a frozen conflict that heavily favored Moscow.[101]

From the start of its incursions into Ukraine, Russia framed the conflict as self-defense against an insidious West that was trying to take Russia's historic territory and add it to its sphere of expansionist influence for capitalist exploitation. Through this lens, Ukraine was merely the latest attempt to attack Russian interests and corrupt the inhabitants of Eastern Europe with decadent consumerism and slavery to neoliberalism, a mere rehash of the same old story. "Russophobia," they call it, implying an instinctive, irrational fear of, and thereby hostility towards, all things Russian.[102] The Ukrainians were traitors, tools of the corrupt West, not to be trusted.

In response, sharp-power measures directed by strongman Putin were called for. Movies were made and funded by the state, like 2015's Battle for Sevastopol, which emphasized the importance of Crimea to Russians by rooting it in the sacrifices of the Second World War. The Night Wolves were mobilized: Zaldostanov and company blockaded roads and worked as a paramilitary force, intimidating and bullying in support of Moscow but allowing for some distance between themselves and the Kremlin. They later put on a spectacular motorcycle show in Crimea for pro-Russian supporters that pulled out all the stops: pyrotechnics, drums, dancing, pro-Stalin poetry readings, two APCs, anti-American puppetry, and even a cameo by Steven Seagal.[103] The Night Wolves portrayed the West as blood-spitting Nazis puppet-controlled by giant cigar-smoking Illuminati-dollar-sign hands, while the Russians and their separatist allies were portrayed as pious, heroic, plucky defenders of a grateful and patriotic fatherland.[104]

THE CONFLICT THAT began with the Maidan demonstrations simmered for years, until Russian troops unexpectedly crossed the border into Ukraine in February 2022 under the

---

101. For a boots-on-the-ground look at the early days of the Ukraine conflict, see Pieniazek, *Greetings from Novorossiya*.

102. See Edwards, "What is Russophobia?"

103. Oh, and motorbikes, too.

104. Seddon, "This Pro-Putin Bike Show Is A Trashy Neo-Soviet 'Triumph Of The Will' Remake."

pretext of squashing Ukrainian pro-Western-ness once and for all. But there is no way Putin expected it to go like this.

At the start of the conflict, the world held its breath. Many experts, even at the highest levels, speculated that something like this might happen as they watched troops amass for months along the border, but few considered it a real possibility. The actual attack stunned observers. It seemed like it was only a matter of time before Russia's superior forces of planes, tanks, and battleships, almost all Soviet kit with a reputation for toughness and reliability, simply crushed any resistance. For those in the West, who had feared Russia's formidable armed forces for decades, it seemed like it was going to be a quick fight. Two hundred thousand Russian troops made straight for Kiev. Russia promised its people and its army a three-day special military operation, a clean in-and-out campaign with little impact on Russian civilians.

Yet, in a twist, the Ukrainian army drove the Russians back from around the capital, and now, over three years after the invasion began, the picture looks very different. The Russian advance has stalled. This failure may stem from Russian incompetence, fostered by decades of systematic corruption and government Potemkinism, as well as Ukrainian tenacity bolstered by billions of dollars' worth of arms and supplies sent by the international community once the initial attack petered out. Who can forget the now-famous images from early in the offensive of out-of-gas Russian tanks clogging Ukrainian highways, or advanced anti-aircraft systems stuck in the mud and towed out by civilian farming tractors?[105]

Following that opening offensive, Russia has focused more on consolidating its hold on the territory in eastern Ukraine it acquired in 2014 and what it claimed in the first weeks. The Russian state began forcibly giving Russian citizenship to residents and, in some cases, relocating them into Russia.[106] The military propped up new, Kremlin-friendly governments in towns like Mariupol and Lysychansk, even though those places were devastated and depopulated by tactics some have described as war crimes. The campaign has worn on, with few major changes to the frontline save the odd offensive here and there. Footage of urban skirmishes, missile strikes, and drone attacks flicker on our screens, but today, it is almost all old news. Both sides seem tired and desperate but unable to stop.[107]

AND SO PUTIN is in a bind. There is no longer an easy out. He has committed too much to retreat, and to call for peace would be to admit defeat, but victory is also out of reach. Russia has been repainted on the international stage as a mean-spirited adolescent bully, made all the more puerile by its apparent inability to follow through on its threats. The simple push that Putin planned has instead become a multi-year meatgrinder. Russia has lost credibility thanks to the sinking of the Russian flagship, missile strikes on civilians, the conscription

---

105. Edwards, "Is This the Plan?"

106. Rodriguez, "Forced Integration through Passportization"; Halladay, "Filtration, Evacuation, Deportation."

107. Edwards, "The Not-too-Mighty Russian Armed Forces."

of prisoners, and a near-coup by private military corporations. North Korean grunts now supplement Russian forces.[108] Putin has become an international pariah. Russia is no longer a world player, an engaged participant at the table. It has become a rogue state, along the lines of Iran or Venezuela.

Meanwhile, internally, Russia is seeing some of the most extreme human rights crackdowns since Stalin's time. A slew of new rules and Orwellian practices were introduced shortly after the invasion began. More than 15,000 protestors were arrested in the first month after the war started as Russians took to the streets. Since then, large, organized protests have mostly fizzled. Some 138,000 websites, including Instagram and Facebook, have been banned in the country. Dozens of media organizations have either closed or been shut down. Individuals speaking out against the war in Ukraine, whether in person or online, risk 15 years in prison. Even celebrities with international clout, such as author Dmitri Glukhovsky, creator of the bestselling Metro book series, have been the target of authorities looking to quash dissent. On August 3, 2022, a State Duma working group published a list of 56 public figures, including political scientists, journalists, and artists, who needed either "education work," had to "repent," or would be forced to resign their positions after expressing displeasure with the Russian government's actions in Ukraine. The state labels their actions "Russophobic" and "extremist."[109] Children are brought into the war, too: veterans visit classrooms to talk about the conflict, youth groups come together to make care packages for soldiers, and units on drone construction and operation have been integrated into the nationwide curriculum.[110] All of this carries the whiff of the same crushing political repression and shrill ideological trumpeting that emanates from the great men of Russian history.

But there are consequences even for the loyal Russian citizen. This may be a war led by Putin and enabled by oligarchs, but everyday Russians are hit hardest. The entirety of the Western world has moved to isolate the Russian economy. Many Western companies have pulled out completely, and international trade has slowed to a trickle thanks to stringent international sanctions. Only food grown in Russia can be sold in the country. As of early 2025, it is estimated that more than half a million Russian troops have died in Ukraine.[111] Many of those who can leave, the wealthy and well-educated, have, further hampering Russia's future. Those remaining are seeing rising prices and an unstable economy.[112]

---

108. Hansler and Britzky, "US says it expects North Korean troops to enter combat against Ukraine in the coming days."

109. Edwards, "Kremlin Cancels Culture."

110. See, for instance, Halladay, "Patriotism Ed"; Friel, "Protection from Propaganda"; and Alebardi, "More Drones in Russian Schools."

111. Government of Ukraine, "How many Russian soldiers have died in Ukraine?"

112. Edwards, "Ghost of Economy Future."

RUSSIA'S TOMORROW LOOKS bleak: military failure, economic hamstringing, and international embarrassment. The Russian people may be hanging on for now, but for how much longer? After 30 years of what looked like maybe, possibly, baby steps towards liberal democracy, Russia has slid back, undoing all its progress. The questions arising now are: Is this all Putin's fault? If so, and if he was taken out of the picture, would things improve? Or is Russia doomed to thrash blindly halfway between a state that simultaneously represents half-hearted democracy and the worst of draconian repression?

Through all of this, though, President Putin remains overwhelmingly popular. One wonders whether this is a result of weeding out dissidents, survey respondents afraid to give their true opinion, or carefully curated media that paints a rosy picture. It is probably a mix of all three.

BUT IT ALL goes back to history. In a speech marking the beginning of the conflict, Putin reveled in the past along the Kremlin's well-worn lines, arguing that, by right, the two states ought to be one under Moscow. The West plundered both Russia and Ukraine in the 1980s and 1990s. NATO expansion threatened both Ukraine and Russia. And Ukrainians should welcome their Russian attackers and forgo the traitorous West because their "fathers, grandfathers, great-grandfathers did not fight the Nazis and defend our common Motherland so that today's Neo-Nazis can seize power in Ukraine. You took an oath of allegiance to the Ukrainian people, and not to the anti-national junta that plunders Ukraine and abuses its people."[113] In short, Russian and Ukrainian history are so intertwined that an independent Ukraine is simply unthinkable. The threat is the same historical threat that has always been there. Ukraine was historically part of Russia, and ought to remain in its sphere of influence, according to the Kremlin. Otherwise, it risks going over to the dark side: the godless West.

Putin's invocation of history has not stopped there. Putin's main justification for his invasion has drawn upon the Putinist retelling of Russia's past. As Rus' was the predecessor to modern Russia, Moscow confidently claims Kiev as its ancient birthright. The Russian claim to the Donbass was cemented by the state media's rechristening of eastern Ukraine as "Novorossiya," digging up the nickname from the 18th century. Putin has repeatedly called the Ukrainian government "Nazis" and "fascists." "Denazification" has been Putin's explicit goal: he accuses the Ukrainian majority of oppressing the Russian minority in eastern regions, despite a lack of evidence to back this up. This is a fight for liberation, he argues, one that Russia has been fighting over and over again since the beginning of its history.[114] And nods to history appear seemingly out of nowhere: Russian soldiers have often been photographed wearing the orange-and-black Ribbon of St. George, which dates from Catherine the Great's time.

---

113. Al Jazeera Staff, "'No other option.'"

114. Edwards, "Searching for Nazis." It is worth noting that in 1936 Adolf Hitler invaded Czechoslovakia saying that he wanted to protect ethnic Germans from oppression at the hands of the Czech state.

In 2023, a new history textbook was released for Russian high schools, covering 1945 to today. It includes the line, "The West has become fixated with destabilizing the situation inside Russia... the aim was not even hidden: to dismember Russia and to get control over its resources." This sentiment is a rehash of classic Putinistic readings of history, playing off the three major themes discussed in the previous chapter, leveraged to legitimize the ongoing conflict.[115]

History is informing and justifying and stirring. It is a Swiss Army knife ready to be deployed for any political task.

RUSSIAN HISTORY STILL fascinates. Its twists and turns are unexpected; its characters are larger than life. It builds upon itself, but its path is far from clear. Perhaps the war in Ukraine is a minor detour. Perhaps it marks a major turning point.

Regardless, thanks to the invasion of Ukraine, almost overnight, Russia has become even more mysterious, even more foreboding to outsiders. There is now a thick curtain hanging around it; travel there is out of the question, and any news coming from Moscow needs to be filtered through for propaganda and bias. It has turned sharply away from Europe and towards its own foreboding stereotypes. As inscrutable as Russia was, it has only become more puzzling.

The only way we can hope to continue to pierce the veil, to try and divine where Russia is heading next, is to look to the past, at the roadmap that has already been made. And with the history being made today, paying attention to the road behind, and how it may influence the road the Kremlin chooses ahead, is more important than ever.

---

115. Faulconbridge, "Kremlin aide rewrites Russian history for a society at war."

EPILOGUE
Why it matters

On November 4, 2016, as the frozen conflict in Ukraine rumbled on, Russia celebrated a newly-reinstituted "Day of Unity." This had been a minor tsarist holiday celebrating Minin and Pozharsky's revolt against Polish invaders, but it was revamped and imbued with new meaning after the start of conflict in Crimea. To mark the holiday, a new statue was unveiled in central Moscow, across a busy street from the Kremlin. It portrayed one of the earliest Russian/Ukrainian heroes: Vladimir I.

In a ceremony bringing together officials from the highest levels of the Russian government and representatives from multiple religions – chiefly Islam, Buddhism, and Christianity – President Putin himself unveiled a massive monument to Vladimir the Great, the famous Baptizer of Rus'. In his speech, Putin stressed the unifying acts of Vladimir and his role as a foundational figure of Russia whose life and times carry valuable lessons for the 21st century: namely, unity through piety in the face of external forces that would seek to undermine or destroy Russia. The president looked to this ancient ruler as the first in the long line of enlightened, strong, sacred rulers, of which Putin himself is only the most recent. This ostensibly interfaith event was closed with Orthodox chanting and prayers.[116]

I was visiting Moscow at the time, there for a few days during a break in study-abroad classes. When I saw a news story that the statue was newly opened, my curiosity was piqued. So, the day after Putin had christened it, I set out from my hostel with a mission. After a quick metro trip, I trudged along a bustling thoroughfare below the Kremlin's red walls, crossing the street at the southwest corner where the new statue was located. I crunched through ice up to the mound where Vladimir stood.

The atmosphere was suddenly reverent, like walking into a silent church sanctuary from a cacophonous city street. Gloomy skies and soft-falling snow seemed to muffle the sounds of passing traffic. A few scattered bunches of other gawkers were poking around. They spoke among themselves quietly. I could not tell if it was out of respect, awe, or awkwardness.

Even with sparse crowds, the monument was imposing. The main figure, which carries a cross-shaped staff in one hand and has his other on a sword at his waist, is nearly sixty feet tall. He is only slightly, but significantly, taller than a counterpart in Kiev. He gazes purposefully

---

116. Press-sluzhba Prezidenta Rossii. "V Den' narodnogo yedinstvo v Moskve otkryt pamiatnik khiaziu Vladimiru."

A snowy Vladimir the Great is baptized by Byzantine priests, conferring on him his role as a defender of Orthodox Christendom. Photo by the author.

in the direction of the Cathedral of Christ the Savior, Moscow's landmark church, now gloriously rebuilt, gleaming in white marble and topped with radiant golden domes that come to the characteristic Russian point. Had original plans gone through for a site on Sparrow Hills behind Moscow State University and above the 1980 Olympics campus, Vladimir's gaze would only have been more commanding, with the glistening whole of the capital and its glittering river at his bronze feet.

Picking my way behind Vladimir's plinth, I discovered three detailed cast-metal panels. They held my attention. Here were scenes from Vladimir's life in relief, set in a modernly manicured garden above an intersection usually clogged with cars and tour buses. These panels remain for me the most intriguing part of the whole artistic ensemble.

His baptism, the middle of three, is the image most steeped in meaning. It is tucked behind, almost hidden, but it is the key to the monument, if not the entirety of modern Russian ideology. To the left, bearded Russian soldiers in Scandinavian-style armor, toting myriad weapons, look on; on the right, robed and sophisticated Byzantine clergy process from the Hagia Sophia (conspicuously missing its Ottoman-era minarets), carrying crosses, a Bible, and a staff with a double-headed eagle. In the middle, under an ancient Russian depiction of the Trinity pulled from medieval icons, Vladimir is solemnly baptized by a priest.

This image is key. This is the creation of Russia, the Third Rome, a combination of deep Slavic militaristic patriotism and Orthodox messianic spirituality, forever preyed on by a hostile West. Byzantine heritage is being literally bestowed on the Russian people. The historical roots of the Ukrainian conflict are summed up, forged in symbols that hint overtly to the sacred mores inherent in the stories of the past. And it is also blatant evidence that it would be impossible to understand the ongoing war without knowing the background, stretching back more than a thousand years, and so hidden (overlooked?) to Western eyes.[117] These are the values Putin was explicitly attempting to preserve with the Ukraine conflict before 2022, and he has only referenced them and clung to them more tightly since.

The conflict is certainly geopolitical. That is clear. But its origins are impenetrable without a weighty historical context informing a robust ideology, working persistently in the background to repurpose ancient symbols for real, modern gains.

RUSSIA'S HISTORY, AND the ideology it informs, is stubbornly distinctive. This distinctiveness means that it is not part of the West and does not want to be part of the West. Its institutions, ideologies, religion, priorities, politics, and economy all differ significantly from what we might consider normal. Russia is unique in the world, and it wants to be unique, and as a result it is so often put at odds with other countries. This is a consequence of the history it tells itself. There can only be one Third Rome.

Understanding how Russia got that way is critical to understanding Russia today. This is why Russia is so profoundly misunderstood: because so few people take into account the full tale, from start to finish, with all the embellishments and emphases added after the fact. When we do look at the whole story, especially the errors and glosses, the picture becomes fuller, its margins and details filled in.

We might not fully understand today's Russia. There are still mysteries and questions frustrating our attempts to fully grasp it. But at least our conception of it can be more comprehensive.

---

117. See further Edwards, "Grand Prince Putin: How and Why Today's Russian State Reminds Us of Its Premodern Past."

Grand Prince Vladimir surveys Moscow traffic. Image by the author.

ACKNOWLEDGMENTS

The main lesson I have learned from hours typing, writing, and rewriting is one of humility. Tens of thousands of words do not appear *ex nihilo*. Instead, this work is a product of three decades of support, nurture, and encouragement from all corners. It is as much due to this inpouring as it is to my outpouring, if not more.

As a child, my family fostered a love of learning. My parents eagerly enabled my voracious reading habits. For all their encouragement and patient support through my education and personal growth, I owe them immeasurable gratitude.

I have had many mentors who steered me towards the study of Russia, its language, and its history. These include trip chaperones, the faculty of my undergraduate and graduate institutions (St. Olaf College and Indiana University), and countless others. Their passion was infectious, and I caught it.

Critically, Paul Richardson of Russian Life shaped this work in many ways, bringing it up to a higher standard than I would have been able to do on my own. He has for years allowed me a space to continue to study Russia as a part-time journalistic editor, giving me a paycheck to keep an eye on Russia. It has been a valuable opportunity to maintain my interest and language skills even as my personal and professional lives have shifted. In addition, he lent crucial insight from his years of Russian history and writing experience to this project. He was also remarkably patient with my repeated check-in emails.

Lastly, I thank my wife and children. My wife for her unending patience and understanding through over a decade of life together. My children for giving me a tangible expression of purpose. They are together a source of unending joy.

BIBLIOGRAPHY

"75% of Russians Say Soviet Era Was 'Greatest Time' in Country's History – Poll." *Moscow Times* March 20, 2020. themoscowtimes.com/2020/03/24/75-of-russians-say-soviet-era-was-greatest-time-in-countrys-history-poll-a69735.

Afanasiev, Alexander. *Russian Fairy Tales*. New York: Pantheon Books, 1945.

AFP. "Russia Bans Insults Against WWII Veterans." *Moscow Times* March 17, 2021. themoscowtimes.com/2021/03/17/russia-bans-insults-against-world-war-ii-veterans-a73274.

Alebardi, Filippo. "More Drones in Russian Schools." *Russian Life* January 2, 2025. russianlife.com/the-russia-file/more-drones-in-russian-schools.

Al Jazeera Staff. "'No other option': Excerpts of Putin's speech declaring war." *Al Jazeera* February 24, 2022. aljazeera.com/news/2022/2/24/putins-speech-declaring-war-on-ukraine-translated-excerpts.

Ascherson, Neal. *Black Sea*. New York: Hill and Wang, 1995.

Assmann, Jan, and John Czaplicka, "Collective Memory and Cultural Identity." *New German Critique* 65 (1995) 125-33.

Bader, Haley. "Don't Cross the Domovoy." *Russian Life* February 7, 2021. russianlife.com/stories/online/dont-cross-the-domovoy/

Beumers, Birgit. *A History of Russian Cinema*. London: Bloomsbury, 2009.

Billington, James H. *The Icon and the Axe: An Interpretive History of Russian Culture*. New York: Alfred A. Knopf, 1968.

Bojanowska, Edyta. *A World of Empires: The Russian Voyage of the Frigate* Pallada. Cambridge, MA: Cambridge University Press, 2018.

Borodin, Alexei. "Pamiatnik Ivanu Groznomu otkryl v Orle." *Interfax.ru* October 14, 2016. interfax.ru/russia/532502.

Caro, Carlo J.V. "Vladimir Putin's 'Orthodoxy, Autocracy, and Nationality.'" University of Pennsylvania Center for Ethics and the Rule of Law, 2022. penncerl.org/the-rule-of-law-post/vladimir-putins-orthodoxy-autocracy-and-nationality.

Chiozza, Giacomo, and Dragomir Stoyanov. "The Myth of the Strong Leader in Russian Public Opinion." *Problems of Post-Communism* 65.6 (2017) 419-33.

Cross, Samuel Hazzard, and Olgerd P. Sherbowitz-Wetzor, eds. and trans. *The Russian Primary Chronicle, Laurentian Text*. Cambridge, MA: Medieval Academy of America, 1953.

D'Andrea, Jeanne, and Stephen West, eds. *The Avant-Garde in Russia 1910-1930: New Perspectives*. Los Angeles: Los Angeles County Museum of Art Press, 1980.

Dunning, Chester S. *Russia's First Civil War: The Time of Troubles and the Founding of the Romanov Dynasty*. University Park, PA: Penn State Press, 2010.

Durkheim, Emile. "From *The Elementary Forms of Religious Life*." In *The Collective Memory Reader*, ed. Jeffrey K. Olick et al. Oxford, UK: Oxford University Press, 2011.

Edele, Mark. *Stalinist Society, 1928-1953*. Oxford, UK: Oxford University Press, 2011.

Edwards, Griffin. "Biking with Style, with Putin: The Night Wolves." *Russian Life* February 6, 2022. russianlife.com/stories/online/biking-with-style-with-putin-the-night-wolves.

—. "Eisenstein's Mythic Masterpiece: Alexander Nevsky." *Russian Life* July 4, 2021. russianlife.com/stories/online/eisensteins-mythic-masterpiece-alexander-nevsky.

—. "The Epic, the Bad, and the Ugly: The Best of Russian History." *Russian Life*, March 4, 2020. russianlife.com/the-russia-file/the-epic-the-bad-and-the-ugly-the-best-of-russian-history/.

—. "The Forgotten Voyage of the Frigate Pallada." *Russian Life* August 29, 2021. russianlife.com/stories/online/the-forgotten-journey-of-the-frigate-pallada.

—. "Ghost of Economy Future." *Russian Life* December 15, 2024. russianlife.com/the-russia-file/ghost-of-economy-future/.

—. "Grand Prince Putin: How and Why Today's Russian State Reminds Us of Its Premodern Past." MA Thesis, University of Indiana, 2021.

—. "Is This the Plan?" *Russian Life* April 7, 2022. russianlife.com/the-russia-file/is-this-the-plan.

—. "Kremlin Cancels Culture." *Russian Life* August 15, 2022. russianlife.com/stories/the-russia-file/kremlin-cancels-culture.

—. "Meet Russia's Newest Meme: Pechenegs." *Russian Life* April 13, 2020. russianlife.com/stories/the-russia-file/meet-russias-newest-meme-pechenegs.

—. "The Not-too-Mighty Russian Armed Forces." *Russian Life* July 24, 2022. russianlife.com/stories/online/the-not-too-mighty-russian-armed-forces.

—. "One for the Books." *Russian Life* May 11, 2025. russianlife.com/the-russia-file/one-for-the-books.

—. "Putin Still Popular." *Russian Life* October 13, 2024. russianlife.com/the-russia-file/putin-still-popular.

—. "Putin's Popularity Perpetuates." *Russian Life* July 20, 2025. russianlife.com/the-russia-file/putins-popularity-perpetuates.

—. "Searching for Nazis." *Russian Life* June 5, 2022. russianlife.com/stories/online/searching-for-nazis.

—. "See Siberia by Train, Virtually." *Russian Life* December 23, 2023. russianlife.com/the-russia-file/see-siberia-by-train-virtually.

—. "Tiger Queen: The Incredible American Odyssey of Rasputin's Daughter." *Russian Life* June 1, 2020. russianlife.com/stories/online/tiger-queen-the-incredible-american-odyssey-of-rasputins-daughter.

—. "What is Russophobia?" *Russian Life* June 8, 2025.

—. "Why Putin Invaded Ukraine." *Russian Life* March 9, 2022. russianlife.com/stories/online/why-putin-invaded-ukraine.

Evtuhov, Catherine. *Portrait of a Russian Province: Economy, Society, and Civilization in Nineteenth-Century Nizhnii Novgorod*. Pittsburgh: University of Pittsburgh Press, 2011.

Fualconbridge, Guy. "Kremlin aide rewrites Russian history for a society at war." *Reuters* August 10, 2023. reuters.com/world/europe/kremlin-aide-rewrites-russian-history-society-war-2023-08-10.

Farquhar, Michael. *Secret Lives of the Tsars: Three Centuries of Autocracy, Debauchery, Betrayal, Murder, and Madness from Romanov Russia*. New York: Random House, 2014.

Fidler, Richard. *Ghost Empire*. New York: HarperCollins, 2016.

Figes, Orlando. *The Crimean War: A History*. New York: Picador, 2010.

"First Monument to Ivan the Terrible Erected in Moscow." *The Moscow Times* July 26, 2017. themoscowtimes.com/2017/07/26/ivan-the-terrible-erected-in-moscow-a58508.

Florinsky, Michael. *The End of the Russian Empire*. New York: Collier, 1961.

Franklin, Simon. "Literacy and Documentation in Early Medieval Russia." *Speculum* 60.1 (1985) 1-38.

Freeze, Gregory L., ed. *Russia: A History*. Oxford: Oxford University Press, 2009.

Friel, Shannon. "Protection from Propaganda: A Back-to-School Essential." *Russian Life* September 7, 2023. russianlife.com/the-russia-file/protection-from-propaganda-a-back-to-school-essential.

Fuller, Willliam C., Jr. *Strategy and Power in Russia, 1600-1914*. New York: The Free Press, 1992.

Garrels, Anne. *Putin Country; A Journey into the Real Russia*. New York: Picador, 2017.

Galstyan, Areg. "Third Rome Rising: The Ideologues Calling for a New Russian Empire." *The National Interest* June 27, 2016. nationalinterest.org/feature/third-rome-rising-the-ideologues-calling-new-russian-empire-1674.

Gilbert, Martin. *The Routledge Atlas of Russian History*. London: Weidenfeld & Nicolson, 1972.

Giles, Kier. *Moscow Rules: What Drives Russia to Confront the West*. Washington, DC: Brookings Institution Press, 2019.

Glasser, Susan. "Putin the Great: Russia's Imperial Impostor." *Foreign Affairs* 98.5 (2019) 10-17.

Goldfrank, David. "Ante-Mongol Rus', Seen from the Top." *Kritika: Explorations in Russian and Eurasian History* 21.1 (Winter 2020) 189-198.

Gorsky, A. A. "K voprosu o sostave russkovo voiska na kulikovom pole." *Newsletter of St. Petersburg State University- History* (2007). http://drevnyaya.ru/vyp/stat/s4_6_3.pdf.

Graeber, David, and David Wengrow. *The Dawn of Everything: A New History of Humanity*. New York: Picador, 2021.

Grey, Ian. "Peter the Great in England." *History Today*. historytoday.com/archive/peter-great-england.

Halbwachs, Maurice. *On Collective Memory*. Translated by Lewis A. Coser. Chicago: University of Chicago Press, 1992.

Halladay, Hannah. "Filtration, Evacuation, Deportation." *Russian Life* May 19, 2022. russianlife.com/the-russia-file/filtration-evacuation-deportation.

—. "Patriotism Ed." *Russian Life* September 20, 2022. russianlife.com/the-russia-file/patriotism-ed.

Halperin, Charles. *Ivan the Terrible: Free to Reward and Free to Punish*. Pittsburgh, PA: University of Pennsylvania Press, 2019.

—. "Novgorod and the 'Novgorodian Land.'" *Cahiers du Monde russe* 40.3 (1999) 345-63.

—. *Russia and the Golden Horde: The Mongol Impact on Medieval Russian History*. Bloomington, IN: Indiana University Press, 1987.

—. "A Tatar interpretation of the battle of Kulikovo Field, 1380: Rustam Nabiev." *Nationalities Papers* 44.1 (2016) 4-19.

—. "Tsarev Ulus: Russia in the Golden Horde." *Cahiers du monde russe et soviétique* 23.2 (April-June 1982) 257-63.

Hansler, Jennifer, and Haley Britzky. "US says it expects North Korean troops to enter combat against Ukraine in the coming days." *CNN.com* November 1, 2024. cnn.com/2024/10/31/politics/us-north-korean-troops-combat-ukraine/index.html.

Hartley, Janet. *The Volga: A History of Russia's Greatest River*. Yale University Press: New Haven, 2021.

Hartog, Eva. "Is Stalin Making a Comeback in Russia?" *The Atlantic* May 28, 2019. theatlantic.com/international/archive/2019/05/russia-stalin-statue/590140.

Hellie, Richard. "Alexander Nevskii's April 5, 1242 Battle on the Ice." *Russian History* 33.2 (Summer-Fall-Winter 2006) 283-87.

Hosking, Geoffrey. *Russia: People and Empire*. Cambridge, MA: Harvard University Press, 1997.

Ibn Fadlan, Ahmad. *Ibn Fadlan and the Land of Darkness: Arab Travellers in the Far North*. New York: Penguin, 2012.

"Indoor Plumbing Still a Pipe Dream for 20% of Russian Households, Reports Say." *Moscow Times* April 2, 2019. themoscowtimes.com/2019/04/02/indoor-plumbing-still-a-pipe-dream-for-20-of-russian-households-reports-say-a65049.

"Ivan the Terrible Monument Vandalized in Russia's Oryol." *The Moscow Times* October 31, 2016. themoscowtimes.com/2016/10/31/ivan-the-terrible-monument-vandalized-a55949.

Ivanov, Sergei. "Rus'-Byzantium-Europe: An Attempt at Triangulation?" *Russian History* 46 (2019) 169-76.

Ivanov, Sergei, Ivan Kurilla, and Adrian Selin. "'Russia: My History': History as an Ideological Tool." *PONARS Eurasia* August 5, 2018. http://ponarseurasia.org/point-counter/russia-my-history-as-ideological-tool.

Ivleva, Marina. "V Vladivostoke otkryt mul'timediinyi Istoricheskii park 'Rossiia: Moia Istoriia'." December 26, 2020. http://vlc.ru/event/news/54323.

Izvestia. "Свыше 78% россиян доверяют Путину." *Iz.ru* November 1, 2024. iz.ru/1784101/2024-11-01/svyshe-78-rossiian-doveriaiut-putinu.

Jenkins, David; Stephanos Alexopoulos; David Bachrach; Jonathan Couser; Sarah Davis; Darin Hayton; and Andrea Sterk, trans. *The Life of St. George of Amastris*. South Bend, IN: Notre Dame University Press, 2001. drive.google.com/file/d/1dgTRTnFhzLb5A0a4kVF005tDU0lpJtvp/view.

Kaimakova, Miliiana; Maciej Salamon; and Małgorzata Smorąg Różycka. *Byzantium, New Peoples, New Powers: The Byzantino-Slav Contact Zone, from the Ninth to the Fifteenth Century*. Krakow, Poland: Towarzystwo Wydawnicze Historia Iagellonica, 2007.

Kaldellis, Anthony. *Byzantium Unbound*. Yorkshire, UK: Arc Humanities, 2019.

Kazhdan, Alexander. "Rus'-Byzantine Princely Marriages in the Eleventh and Twelfth Centuries." *Harvard Ukrainian Studies* 12.13 (1988-1989) 414-29.

Khlevniuk, Oleg. *Stalin: New Biography of a Dictator*. New Haven, CT: Yale University Press, 2015.

Khrushcheva, Nina L. "No Heads Are Better Than Two." *Foreign Policy* December 19, 2009. foreignpolicy.com/2009/12/19/no-heads-are-better-than-two.

Kivelson, Valerie A., and Ronald Suny. *Russia's Empires*. New York: Oxford University Press, 2017.

Kononov, A. *Stories about Lenin*. Moscow: Foreign Language Publishing House, 1944.

Langer, Lawrence. "Muscovite Taxation and the Problem of Mongol Rule in Rus'." *Russian History* 34, 1 (2007): 101-29.

—. "The 'Strangeness' of Rus' in the Mongol Era." *Russian History / Histoire Russe* 21.1 (2001) 273-94.

Laruelle, Marlene. *Is Russia Fascist?: Unraveling Propaganda East and West*. Ithaca: Cornell University Press, 2021.

Lavrov, Sergei. "Russian Foreign Policy in a Historical Perspective." *Russia in Global Affairs*. March 3, 2016. eng.globalaffairs.ru/number/Russias-Foreign-Policy-in-a-Historical-Perspective-18067.

Lenhoff, Gail. "Rus'-Tatar Princely Marriages in the Horde: The Literary Sources." *Russian History* 42.1 (2015) 16-31.

Lenhoff, Gail, and Janet Martin. "Marfa Boretskaia, Posadnitsa of Novgorod: A Reconsideration of Her Legend and Her Life." *Slavic Review* 59.2 (2000) 343-68.

Levada Center. "Dynamika otnosheniya k Stalinu." *Levada.ru* April 16, 2019. levada.ru/2019/04/16/dinamika-otnosheniya-k-stalinu.

Lieven, Dominic, ed. *The Cambridge History of Russia, Volume 2: Imperial Russia, 1689-1917*. Cambridge, UK: Cambridge University Press, 2006.

Maiorov, Alexander V. "Byzantine Purple in Ancient Rus'." *Kritika: Explorations in Russian and Eurasian History* 20.3 (Summer 2019) 505-27.

Martin, Janet. "The Land of Darkness and the Golden Horde: The Fur Trade under the Mongols, XIIIth-XIVth Centuries." *Cahiers du monde russe et soviétique* 19.4 (1978) 401-21.

Massie, Robert K. *Peter the Great: His Life and World*. New York: Ballantine Books, 1981.

May, Timothy. *The Mongol Art of War: Chinggis Khan and the Mongol Military System*. Havetown, PA: Casemate Publishers, 2007.

—. *The Mongol Conquests in World History*. London: Reaktion Books, 2012.

Medvedev, Sergei. *A War Made in Russia*. Cambridge, UK: Polity Press, 2023.

Merridale, Catherine. *Lenin on the Train*. New York: Picador, 2017.

—. *Red Fortress: History and Illusion in the Kremlin*. New York: Metropolitan, 2013.

Miles, Jonathan. *St. Petersburg: Madness, Murder, and Art on the Banks of the Neva*. New York: Pegasus Books, 2018.

Mongait, Alexandr. *Archaeology in the USSR*. New Orleans: Pelican, 1962.

Morgan, David. *The Mongols*. Hoboken, NJ: John Wiley & Sons, Inc, 1986.

Navalny, Alexei. "Putin's palace. History of world's largest bribe." *Youtube* January 19, 2021. youtube.com/watch?v=ipAnwilMncI.

Nelson, James Carl. *The Polar Bear Expedition*. New York: HarperCollins, 2019.

Nora, Pierre. *Realms of Memory: Rethinking the French Past*. Translated by Arthur Goldhammer. New York: Columbia University Press, 1998.

Norwich, James Julius. *A Short History of Byzantium*. New York: Vintage Books, 1997.

NPR Staff. "Bones and Grooves: The Weird Secret History of Soviet X-Ray Music." *NPR* January 9, 2016. npr.org/2016/01/09/462289635/bones-and-grooves-weird-secret-history-of-soviet-x-ray-music.

Obolensky, Dmitri. *The Byzantine Commonwealth: Eastern Europe, 500-1453*. Westport, CT: Greenwood, 1971.

Ostrovsky, Arkady. *The Invention of Russia: From Gorbachev's Freedom to Putin's War*. New York: Viking, 2015.

Paul, Michael. "'A Man Chosen by God': The Office of Archbishop in Novgorod, Russia (1165-1478)." PhD Diss., University of Miami, 2003.

—. "Was The Prince of Novgorod a 'Third-Rate Bureaucrat' after 1136?" *Jahrbücher für Geschichte Osteuropas* 56.1 (2008): 72-113.

Pieniazek, Pawel. *Greetings from Novorossiya: Eyewitness to the War in Ukraine*. Pittsburgh: University of Pittsburgh Press, 2017.

Perrie, Maureen, ed. *The Cambridge History of Russia, Volume 1: From Early Rus' to 1689*. Cambridge, UK: Cambridge University Press, 2006.

Plokhy, Serhii. *Lost Kingdom: The Quest for Empire and the Birth of the Russian Nation*. New York: Basic Books, 2017.

Pravoslavie.ru. "The Fall of an Empire: The Lesson of Byzantium." *YouTube* November 15, 2012. youtube.com/watch?v=f1CWG-2GLU4.

Press-sluzhba Prezidenta Rossii. "V Den' narodnogo yedinstvo v Moskve otkryt pamiatnik khiaziu Vladimiru." *Kremlin.ru* November 6, 2016. http://kremlin.ru/events/president/news/53211/photos.

Prestel, David. "Kievan Rus' Theology: Yes, No, and It Depends." *Russian History* 46 (2019) 177-92.

"Putin unveils 'provocative' Moscow statue of St Vladimir." *BBC.com* November 4, 2016. bbc.com/news/world-europe-37871793.

Rappaport, Helen. *Caught in the Revolution*. New York: St. Martin's Press, 2016.

Rapport, Mike. *The Napoleonic Wars: A Very Short Introduction*. Oxford, UK: Oxford University Press, 2013.

Renan, Ernest. "What is a Nation?" Sorbonne. 1882. Lecture. http://ucparis.fr/files/9313/6549/9943/What_is_a_Nation.pdf.

Rice, Condoleeza. *Democracy: Stories from the Long Road to Freedom*. New York; Twelve Press, 2017.

Robinson, Paul. *Russian Conservatism*. Ithaca: Cornell University Press, 2019.

Rodriguez, Rachel. "Forced Integration through Passportization." *Russian Life* May 29, 2022. russianlife.com/the-russia-file/forced-integration-through-passportization.

Rosenberg, Steve. "What a new Stalin statue says about Russia's attempt to reshape history." *BBC.com* May 28, 2025. bbc.com/news/videos/cz63n6j7407o.

"Rossiia: Moia Istoriia." *MyHistoryPark.ru*. myhistorypark.ru.

Sanborn, Joshua A. *Imperial Apocalypse: The Great War & the Destruction of the Russian Empire*. Oxford, UK: Oxford University Press, 2014.

Schmemann, Serge. "Gorbachev Freed the Soviet Union but Could Not Save It." *The New York Times* August 31, 2022. nytimes.com/2022/08/31/opinion/gorbachev-death-soviet-union.html.

Seddon, Max. "This Pro-Putin Bike Show Is A Trashy Neo-Soviet 'Triumph Of The Will' Remake." *Buzzfeed* August 11, 2014.

Sevanstyanova, Olga. "In Quest of the Key Democratic Institution of Medieval Rus': Was the 'Veche' an Institution that Represented Novgorod as a City and a Republic?" *Jahrbücher für Geschichte Osteuropas* 58.1 (2010) 1-23.

Shamanska, Anna. "Bloody Stake: 'Alternative' Monument To Ivan The Terrible Unveiled In Russia." *Radio Free Europe / Radio Liberty* October 24, 2016.

Shirnina, Amanda. "The Tsar with the Dragon Tattoo." *Russian Life* May 4, 2021. russianlife.com/stories/the-russia-file/the-tsar-with-the-dragon-tattoo.

"Skazanie o bitve Novgorodtsev s Suzdal'tsami." *Elektronnye publikatsii* 2011. http://lib.pushkinskijdom.ru/Default.aspx?tabid=4993.

Smele, Jonathan D. *The "Russian" Civil Wars, 1916-1926: Ten Years That Shook the World*. New York: Oxford University Press, 2017.

Southgate, Vix. *Dogs in Space: The Amazing True Story of Belka and Strelka*. New York: Wren & Rook, 2018.

Stathakopoulos, Dionysios. *A Short History of the Byzantine Empire*. New York: Bloomsbury, 2014.

Steinbeck, John. *A Russian Journal, with Photographs by Robert Capa*. London: Penguin Classics, 1999.

Sunderland, Willard. *The Baron's Cloak: A History of the Russian Empire in War and Revolution*. Ithaca: Cornell University Press, 2014.

Suny, Ronald Grigor, ed. *The Cambridge History of Russia, Volume 3: The Twentieth Century*. Cambridge, UK: Cambridge University Press, 2006.

Thompson, Andrea. "Volcano in 1600 caused global disruption." *NBC News* May 5, 2008. nbcnews.com/id/wbna24467948.

Tsouras, Peter. "'The Fury of the Northmen': Viking Assault on Constantinople, 860." *HistoryNet.com* May 2014. historynet.com/the-fury-of-the-northmen-viking-assault-constantinople-860.htm.

Ukrainian government. "How many Russian soldiers have died in Ukraine?" November 1, 2024. war.ukraine.ua/faq/what-are-the-russian-death-toll-and-other-losses-in-ukraine.

Vock, Ido. "Tucker Carlson interview: Fact-checking Putin's 'nonsense' history." *BBC.com* February 9, 2024. bbc.com/news/world-europe-68255302.

Walker, Christopher. "What Is 'Sharp Power'?" *Journal of Democracy* 29.3 (July 2018) 9-23. journalofdemocracy.org/articles/what-is-sharp-power.

Walker, Shaun. "From one Vladimir to another: Putin unveils huge statue in Moscow." *The Guardian* November 4, 2016.

X (formally George Kennan). "The Sources of Soviet Conduct." *Foreign Affairs* 25.4 (July 1947) 566-82.

Zenkovsky, Serge, ed. *Medieval Russia's Epics, Chronicles, and Tales*. New York: Meridian, 1974.

ABOUT THE AUTHOR

Griffin Edwards is a writer and editor based in Eugene, Oregon. He earned his master's degree in Russian and East European studies from Indiana University Bloomington and since 2021 has been managing digital editor for *Russian Life* magazine.

www.ingramcontent.com/pod-product-compliance
Lightning Source LLC
Chambersburg PA
CBHW071205070526
44584CB00019B/2924